Mind Frames

Warren Henderson

Mind Frames
By Warren Henderson
Copyright ©2004

Published by Gospel Folio Press
304 Killaly Street West
Port Colborne, ON, L3K 6A6, Canada
ISBN 1-882701-94-1

ORDERING INFORMATION:
Gospel Folio Press
Phone 1-905-835-9166
E-mail: orders@gospelfolio.com

Printed in the United States of America

Contents

Acknowledgements

"For the body is not one member, but many" (1 Cor. 12:14).
Those within the body of Christ enjoy equality and privilege
beyond any social order or human institution. Each member of
the Church is divinely equipped and enabled to serve the body
as appointed by God. It is for this reason that the author is
deeply indebted to all those who sacrificed their time and tal-
ents to aid the publishing of Mind Frames. I thank the Lord for
each of the following and their contributions: Jabe and John
Nicholson for cover design and layout. Jabe Nicholson, David
Dunlap, and Mike Attwood for technical editing. Caroline
Cairns, and Jane Biberstein for general editing. Karen Cyboski,
Gina Mulligan, Annette Hanson, and my lovely wife Brenda for
proofreading assistance.

Introduction to Mind Frames

Prolonged exposure to the frigid conditions of a Midwestern blizzard can be life threatening, yet from the security of your home this majestic scene is intriguing and harmless. Snowflakes scurry along a shifting canopy of snow while overhead trees batter each another for territorial rights. Through a window one may view the fierce reality of the storm without experiencing its harsh consequences. Two senses penetrate through the window to verify the existence of the storm, namely sight and hearing. When one presses their hand against the glass of the window a third sense is invoked and instantly more awareness of outside circumstance is gained. A stinging chill fastens to the fingers and palm. In an instant the mind determines the uncomfortable sensation and commands the hand to withdraw from the chilling glass.

Similarly, the human soul is a window that connects two radically diverse realms. The soul is a living portal between the spiritual and physical realms, a connection amid the seen and unseen. Through this window God may express His mind to a fallen world even while it is under the delegated control of Satan.

God, who is triune, created man in His image. Man is not God, nor triune, but tripartite. God is three distinct persons (Father, Son and Spirit), while man is one person with three parts (spirit, soul and body). The human components are interrelated, but are exclusive in their properties. The Holy

Spirit acknowledges man's physiological design of spirit, soul, and body (1 Thess. 5:23). The body is "world-conscious," the soul is "self-conscious," and the spirit of man is "God-conscious." The spirit is the noblest part of man and refers to the innermost area of our being – the "inner man." The body is the lowest portion of our existence and forms the outermost being. Between these two components dwells the soul. The soul comprises our intellect, our emotions, our personality, and our will. Through the five senses the soul links with the physical realm, and through the spirit the soul connects with God. The soul is a bridge, a window, a medium set between the body and the spirit. When a believer is in fellowship with God, the Holy Spirit has freedom to commune with man's spirit, which transmits godly thoughts to the soul. This in turn exercises the body to conform to the Spirit's rule. In this way a believer becomes a vessel fit for the infusing power of the Spirit with all of God's goodness rushing through his/her entire being.

Before the fall of man, Adam's soul was completely under the control of his spirit. He was upright and innocent, and in direct communion with the Holy Spirit (Eccl. 7:29). But the spirit cannot act directly upon the body without the medium of the soul. Thus, the will of man can choose to ignore his spirit and follow the baser desires of the body. God created the soul of man to stand between and exercise power over the whole of man to discern and to determine to pursue the spiritual rather than the natural world. The soul of man includes his heart, will, and mind. The mind is the intellectual and cognitive center of the soul and, thus, ultimately discerns the direction the soul will follow. The mind is, therefore, a frame that constrains the soul in the same manner that a window frame constrains the glass. In both cases an entrance between two realities is formed. Watchman Nee summarizes this reality:

The soul makes it possible for the spirit and the body to communicate and to cooperate. The work of the soul is to keep these two in their proper order so that they may not lose their right relationship–namely, that the lowest, the body, may be subjected to the spirit, and that the highest, the spirit, may govern the body through the soul. Man's prime factor is definitely the soul. It looks to the spirit to give what the latter has received from the Holy Spirit in order that the soul, after it has been perfected, may transmit what it has obtained to the body; then the body too may share in the perfection of the Holy Spirit and so become a spiritual body.[1]

The bulk of scriptural exhortation is not focused upon the soul, or the heart, but upon the mind. Thus, the mind must be "transformed" (Rom. 12:2) in order to "form" a pure heart (Ps. 51:10). A pure heart serves to "conform"(Eph. 6:5-8) the will to God's will. The mind is clearly the locale between the physical and spiritual realms where spiritual battles are won or lost. The mind frames the soul's will and emotions. If a believer truly desires the Holy Spirit to have free access through his soul window, the mind must be properly framed. This book identifies scriptural mind frames that, when applied, will allow the Holy Spirit to have free recourse through the soul – free access to affect Christ-likeness in the physical realm. If the mind is framed properly, the soul becomes a funnel extended to heaven by which spiritual blessings freely flow to earth. In this sense, a proper scriptural mind frame provides a corridor for the Holy Spirit to impose spiritual power to battle evil in the world through human agents (He literally hinders sin – 2 Thess. 2:7).

The Lord Jesus decreed, *"And thou shalt love the Lord thy God with all thy heart, and with all thy soul, and with **all thy mind**, and with all thy strength: this is the first commandment"* (Mk. 12:30). Dear reader, does the Lord have your **whole** mind? Who or what controls your mind? If you love the Lord with your entire mind, your heart and body will be constrained to do the same.

In the resurrection, the spirit of the believer will completely rule his or her glorified body, for the physical body will be raised a spiritual body (1 Cor. 15:44). Why wait for the resurrection when the resurrected life of Christ is available now for all to witness and enjoy? What is the purpose of Christ's redemption? Why did He suffer so much on our behalf? His desire is that all hindrances of our fallen state might be eliminated, thus, allowing the Holy Spirit total and unrestricted control of our whole person. In this we truly become spiritual persons and obtain the capacity to please and express thanksgiving to our Savior. To the glory and delight of God, we progress towards Christ-likeness.

If the reader has difficulty maintaining a spiritual thought life, or is ineffective in spiritual warfare, or is prone to repetitive carnal behavior, this book is for you. It is the author's sincerest prayer that through imposing scriptural "mind frames" the reader will obtain a fortified mind and be an effective portal for the Holy Spirit's power in a world that desperately needs God's presence!

> The gracious and faithful man obtains more grace and more means of usefulness, while the unfaithful man sinks lower and lower and grows worse and worse. We must either make progress or else lose what we have attained. There is no such thing as standing still in religion.
>
> Charles Haddon Spurgeon

God's Icon

Since human history has been recorded, mankind has always been fascinated with himself – from where did we originate, and how do we exist?

Many early church theologians were adversely influenced by Greek philosophy in their understanding of what it meant to be created in the "image of God" (Gen. 1:26). The Greeks generally understood a human dualism and, thus, drew a complete separation between the physical and the spiritual components. They believed a person was an individual spirit existing in a living body, much the way we might choose to reside in a tent during a camping trip. Through the latter centuries of the church age theologians rejected dualism to battle over whether individuals are composed of only body and soul, or of body, soul, and spirit. Regardless of your thinking on this matter, man is plainly composed of an outer self that relates to the world through fives senses, and an inner self which thinks, has emotions and a will.

But what does the Bible declare about who we are? Can we understand our existence? Vernon O. Elmore responds to these questions:

> The Bible portrays them [humans] as self-conscious, willful, innovative entities who, under God, preside over their environment. In other words, they are persons. God

made each male and female a person in the likeness of His own personhood. Nothing else in all creation can be called a person. Personhood encompasses individuals in their entirety, body and spirit, as rational, loving, responsible, moral creatures.[1]

The Creation of Man

Much of what God reveals to us about our origin, purpose, and essence is contained in the book of Genesis.

And God said, Let us make man in our image, after our likeness: and let them have dominion over the fish of the sea, and over the fowl of the air, and over the cattle, and over all the earth, and over every creeping thing that creepeth upon the earth. So God created man in his own image, in the image of God created he him; male and female created he them (Gen 1:26-27).

And the LORD God formed man of the dust of the ground, and breathed into his nostrils the breath of life; and man became a living soul (Gen. 2:7).

Man was created in God's image, but what does the word "image" imply? The Greek word for "image" is *eikon*. The root meaning of e*ikon* is derived from the word *eiko,* which means "be like or to resemble." The literal meaning of *eikon* is "likeness," but in the figurative sense, it means "a representation." Our English word "icon" is derived from *eikon*. Icons have become a common part of computer operating systems. The user is able to click on an icon to initiate or to open a desired program or file. The icon is not the program or file, but is an image that represents the program or file. Paul implies by the use of *eikon* in 1 Corinthians 11:7 that man was made in the moral likeness of God and that man figuratively "represents" God. Adam was not God, but he was an icon representing Him.

Adam did not become a living "soul" apart from a physical body or the life-giving breath of God (Gen. 2:7; 1 Cor. 15:45). Body, soul, and spirit are not opposing terms, but rather supplementing dimensions that together describe aspects of the inseparable whole person. Originally, Adam had a soul similar to that of an angel in that he was created innocent, possessed personhood (individuality), and could freely exercise moral choice (Eccl. 7:29; Gen. 3:6). Yet, Adam's outward man more resembled created animals than spiritual heavenly beings. But what differentiated him from all other created things? He alone was created in God's image and, thus, represented God in this New World. His created position was higher than all creatures who call earth home, yet lower than those spiritual beings of God's habitation (Heb. 2:7-8). As God's representative, he was to rule over the earth (Gen. 1:28, 2:19).

Before the fall of mankind, Adam and Eve enjoyed a life of felicity and harmony with their Creator. Feelings of significance and security permeated every fiber of their being. They felt significant because they were fulfilling God's intended purpose for them: to keep His garden (Gen. 2:15), to exercise authority over the creatures of the earth, and in God's timing to procreate. As all their physical, emotional, and spiritual needs were amply provided, a deep sense of security characterized their existence. Man and his Creator walked hand in hand. Man's spirit completely ruled his mind. The human "will" knew only to do what God had decreed, and his emotions were a replica of his Creator's. His flesh had no control over his mind, other than what was normal in creation order. All was at peace. On the sixth day of creation, God miraculously raised up an icon from the dust of the earth to be His crowning finale

(Heb. 2:7). Adam gleamed as a perfect representative of his God.

Man after the Fall

God had informed Adam shortly after his creation, *"But of the tree of the knowledge of good and evil, thou shalt not eat of it: for in the day that thou eatest thereof thou shalt surely die"* (Gen. 2:17). Life was wonderful until that horrible day that changed the course of humanity forever. Satan externally solicited Adam and Eve to do evil, and they chose to believe the "father of lies" instead of the Father of all.

The same satanic deception and desire for knowledge presently blinds many from heeding the truth that would liberate their souls from the bondage of sin. As C. H. Spurgeon put it, "Be on guard today that the tree of knowledge does not keep you from the tree of life."

Our first parents listened to seducing words instead of the quiet voice of their spirits. Paul informs us that Eve was deceived and that Adam knowingly followed the lead of his wife and sinned (1 Tim. 2:13-14). Adam sinned with his "eyes open." God held his representative, Adam, directly accountable for the error (Rom. 5:12). Just as God said, mankind died that day and would continually die. Adam and his wife experienced spiritual death the moment the sin was committed. They would gradually die physically, their bodies eventually returning to the ground from which man came.

Although several types of death are spoken of in Scripture, there are three deaths or "separations" that are most significant to all mankind. As a result of Adam's sin, we are all born **spiritually dead**; we are spiritually separated from God. Then, when **physical death** occurs, our soul separates from our body (Lk. 16:22-23; 2 Cor. 5:8). If physical death occurs while still being spiritually dead, **eternal death** is assured (eternal judgment in hell). Hebrews 9:27 proclaims, *"That it is appointed unto man once to die, but after this the judgment."* The only exception to the above is that perhaps God will demonstrate His grace by applying the blood of Christ to those infants who died in the womb or early in life, before they understood the moral law within them and God's solution to their sin problem. Perhaps the mentally handicapped will be made trophies of God's grace in the same way. But as adults and older children, the unsaved are just one heartbeat, one breath away from sealing their eternal woe.

Adam and the woman's fellowship with God was severed. They now felt uneasy with God and even tried to hide from His presence. Billows of guilt and waves of shame relentlessly pounded their awakened conscience. The anguish of impending judgment swept over them like a flood. God would judge them and thrust them out of the garden to struggle for survival on a cursed planet. Instead of significance, they felt rejection. Gone too was their security; they were now on their own, having to rely on their own strength and self-control to live. In a brief moment their secure and significant communion with God was forfeited. Now feelings of rejection, shame, and helplessness overwhelmed them. Suddenly, many new choices became available. The human spirit no longer ruled the mind, which had successfully maintained the emotions and the will of man in check. The flesh soon bombarded the mind with base lusts and wanton desires. The immensity of that moment for our first parents was staggering. The spirit of man would continue to speak within, but the competition to be heard suddenly became fierce.

Even now, it is our spirit that confesses to our soul that there is a God and life after death. During a nighttime stroll, man will invariably gaze heavenward, and while beholding the starry host upon a canopy of blackness, a voice deep within him whispers, "There is Someone out there – there is a God."

Our human spirit needs God and communion with Him to be satisfied. Being impoverished of two senses, a blind and deaf Helen Keller acknowledges eloquently what her spirit cries out from within, "I believe in the immortality of the soul because I have within me immortal longings."

It is only through man's spirit that worship can be rendered to God (Phil. 3:3). Consequently, at the spirit level of man resides his most intense need – to be one with his Creator. Many will try to fill this void with momentary thrills that satisfy the lusts of the flesh such as drugs, amusements, and unlawful sex; or venture after the more sophisticated fascinations of the soul – fame, power, intellect, and wealth. What temporal stimulus could ever satisfy man's deepest spiritual need to be one with his Creator? None.

> If God should give my soul all He ever made or might make, apart from Himself, and giving it, He stayed away even by as much as a hairbreadth, my soul would not be satisfied.
>
> Meister Eckhart

> So it is that men sigh on, not knowing what the soul wants, but only that it needs something. Our yearnings are homesickness for heaven. Our sighings are sighings for God just as children that cry themselves to sleep away from home and sob in their slumber, not knowing that they sob for their parents. The soul's inarticulate moanings are the affections, yearning for the Infinite, and having no one to tell them what it is that ails them.
>
> Henry Ward Beecher

Though "the flesh" sometimes refers to the human body, it is applied especially in the epistles to refer to the fallen independent nature which allows sin its opportunity within us. John explains that the "lusts of the flesh" did not come from God, but from the world – a system under Satan's delegated control and apart from God (1 Jn. 2:16). Man, in his fallen state, will struggle to find meaning in life independent from God. Life is meaningless without God, thus the sum total of man's pursuing will be characterized by feelings of insecurity, inadequacy, anxiety, and guilt. The natural man may think that he is at liberty to choose his behavior, but since he possesses a fallen nature, he invariably must walk according to the flesh and commit the "deeds of the flesh" listed in Galatians 5:19-21. Paul speaks of the warring of two natures within the believer, the flesh (independent and selfish desires) and the Spirit nature (through our human spirit). The natural man sins naturally, but the believer chooses to sin, when he or she ignores the Holy Spirit's direction.

There is therefore now no condemnation to them which are in Christ Jesus, who walk not after the flesh, but after the Spirit. For the law of the Spirit of life in Christ Jesus hath made me free from the law of sin and death. For what the law could not do, in that it was weak through the flesh, God sending his own Son in the likeness of sinful flesh, and for sin, condemned sin in the flesh: That the righteousness of the law might be fulfilled in us, who walk not after the flesh, but after the Spirit. For they that are after the flesh do mind the things of the flesh; but they that are after the Spirit the things of the Spirit. For to be carnally minded is death; but to be spiritually minded is life and peace. Because the carnal mind is enmity against God: for it is not subject to the law of God,

> *neither indeed can be. So then they that are in the flesh*
> *cannot please God* (Rom. 8:1-8).

It is the spirit of man, specifically the conscience, that produces feelings of guilt when we transgress the moral law God planted within us (Jas. 4:17). Only the spirit of man can explain the internal feelings of impending judgment we realize after confronting our own conscience. Natural man cannot identify the source of these intense feelings. What can be done to quiet the deafening apprehension of a wounded conscience? Pondering his loathsome situation, man rationalizes, "If doing something I know to be wrong induced mental fatigue, then doing what I know to be right should ease my guilty pangs." The evolutionists have difficulty explaining these natural and unlearned facets of our being. Each of us, to some degree, instinctively knows right and wrong. This explains why cultures of the world (even isolated societies) generally possess a similar code of social ethics – it is wrong to murder, steal, commit adultery, etc.

As a result, except for Christianity, the religions of the world are founded on the "need of doing" to obtain a supernatural blessing. A works-based religion is the natural product of a depraved human conscience. Paul successfully argues that man proves to himself, by his grieving conscience, that he is a sinner (Rom. 2:1-16). The fact that we feel guilt is evidence that we did not continue in well doing; we did not obey what we instinctively knew was appropriate behavior (Rom. 2:15). Thus we prove to ourselves that we are sinners; that we fall below the perfect standard of righteousness needed to enter heaven (Rom. 3:23).

Christianity declares that you cannot "do" something to earn your way to heaven – you could never do enough, and what is necessary to gain entrance has already been "done" at Calvary. The world's religion cries "do," while Christianity declares "done." Consequently, we must realize that our body, soul, and spirit, yes, every aspect of our being has been affected adversely by sin, and only through Jesus Christ and the power of the Holy Spirit can the matter be resolved.

Dividing Asunder Soul and Spirit

Most of us have likely enrolled in at least one biology class at some time or another. Eventually, with scalpel clutched in trembling hand, we carefully divided a frog, or cat, or some other pale formaldehyde-soaked creature to expose its inner formerly functioning parts. From external observation no one could have fathomed the complexity of the inner workings necessary to sustain physical life. Science has discovered that the vital systems needed to maintain a living organism are distinct from one another, yet vitally linked in operation and crucially dependent on one another. Though the absence of some functions such as the nervous or cardiovascular systems usher in death more expediently than a dysfunctional digestive system, the result is the same – life ends.

Not only is each living organism composed of visibly distinct and inter-connected life-sustaining systems, each also possesses invisible spheres of consciousness, with the more sophisticated life forms demonstrating the capacity of emotions and thought. These inner qualities are similarly distinct, but are inter-connected capacities to ensure the continuation of life. What is seen in life about us arouses curiosity as to what cannot be observed through a microscope. We yield to the fact that what is verified by our senses in the physical realm is but a mere pattern of what is not seen. Scripture also reveals this same fascinating link amid spiritual and temporal qualities.

The tabernacle, with its furnishings, was an elementary model of God's unseen majestic temple in heavenly realms (Heb. 9:23). The Old Testament is packed full of visible pictures-shadows and types of the yet forthcoming Savior and His future redemptive work. These bore testimony of a future reality, but when prophetically dispensed were illusive of substance. Since there is unimaginable complexity in the inner working of the visible portions of our bodies, we may also assume the unseen portion is similarly complex. What is the invisible working portion of our being?

Modern psychology and sociology represent man's best attempts to define through observation and experimentation man's hidden self. Thus, monitored behavior becomes the exclusive component for humanistic theories. Yet, these sciences must neglect portions of human composition or admit that there is a Master Designer – a Creator. A college student recently informed me that his university psychology teacher declared on the first day of class, "I will prove to you this semester that you do not have a soul and that there is no God." Ignored in these humanistic sciences is the study of the soul and spirit of man, which are eternal (Job 19:26; Eccl. 12:7; Matt. 22:32), and the inclusion of moral qualities, which are monitored by a built-in protection system called a "conscience" (Rom. 2:15). To admit man has a "built-in" moral standard and an immortal quality is to affirm a divine standard of righteousness and an eternal Creator, through whom life continues to exist. What does the Bible say concerning the essence of man? Holman's Bible Dictionary provides the following comments concerning human essence:

> ... a human being is a totality of being, not a combination of various parts and impulses. According to the Old Testament understanding, a person is not a body which

happens to possess a soul. Instead, a person is a living soul. Genesis 2:7 relates God forming man "of dust from the ground" and breathing into his nostrils "the breath of life." (See Jer. 18:6.) The man became human when God breathed the breath of life. Because of God's activity, humanity became a special and unique part of creation. Because of God's breath of life, the man became "a living being" (Gen. 2:7). A person, thus, is a complete totality, made up of human flesh, spirit (best understood as "the life-force"), and *nephesh* (best understood as "the total self" but often translated as "soul"). Human flesh cannot exist alone. Neither can spirit or *nephesh* [soul] exist alone. Together, however, they comprise a complete person.[1]

Often in the Old Testament, and occasionally in the New Testament, the terms *soul* and *spirit* are used interchangeably. However, the New Testament clearly endorses a distinction between the body, soul, and spirit of man.

> *And the very God of peace sanctify you wholly; and I pray God your whole **spirit and soul and body** be preserved blameless unto the coming of our Lord Jesus Christ* (1 Thess. 5:23).

> *For the word of God is living, and powerful, and sharper than any two-edged sword, piercing even to the **dividing asunder of soul and spirit**, and of the joints and marrow, and is a discerner of **the thoughts [mind]** and intents of **the heart*** (Heb. 4:12).

> *For as the body without the spirit is dead, so faith without works is dead also* (Jas. 2:26).

Yet these elements of our inner human existence must be viewed as dimensions of the same life. Every physical object must have height, length, and width to exist; likewise our being is composed of body, soul, and spirit. Scripture does not represent people as individuals composed of distinct parts, but as integrated beings capable of interacting with others. We were created in God's image. Therefore, just as God is a unity, man is also a unity. Each of these three dimensions of our existence (body, soul, and spirit) also enables three distinct realms of consciousness. The "body" is *flesh*, or more broadly, *world*-conscious, the "soul" is *self*-conscious, and the "spirit" is *God*-conscious.

The Body

In the New Testament the word "body" is derived from the Greek word *soma* and speaks of the physical shape or form of a person. The body is temporal – its creation is initiated at conception, and it rapidly deteriorates after the soul separates from it at death. The "body" is conscious of the basic necessities of life: hunger, thirst, fatigue, warmth, and sexual gratification. These desires are coordinated through the five senses (sight, taste, hearing, smell, touch) to the soul dimension. Or as Joseph Joubert poetically explains, "The ears and eyes are the doors and windows of the soul."[2]

The Soul

The Hebrew word *nephesh* is used 755 times in the Old Testament to refer to human beings (i.e souls). Hence, *nephesh* may be translated either "soul," "life," "person" or, on rare occasions, "body," usually in reference to a dead person. The English language commonly interchanges these terms as well. For example, it may be said, "The ship sank in the North Atlantic, and all souls were lost." The reference is not to the human soul exclusively, but to the whole person. The Greek term related to *nephesh* is *psuche* (from which *psyche* is derived) which refers to the "total self." For example, the Lord Jesus told His disciples, *"I am the Good Shepherd; the Good Shepherd giveth His **life** for the sheep"* (Jn. 10:11). The Lord Jesus was compelled as the Good Shepherd to sacrifice His *total self* for His sheep. *Psuche* is translated "life" in this verse. *Psuche* is the only Greek word rendered "soul" in the entire New Testament. The soul is actually the animated and natural life of man. Without the soul there is no existence. It is possible to exist after death without a body (2 Cor. 5:8; Mk. 12:27; Rev. 6:9), and it is possible to exist presently and ignore the influence of the human spirit (Rom. 1:28; 1 Cor. 2:14; 1 Tim. 4:12). But to live one must have a soul, it cannot be ignored or cease to exist. Thus, the life of man is the soul permeating a body.

Every "soul" is unique, and is what ensures that you are you (a distinct individual from everyone else). The soul expresses the entire personality (Ps. 33:20) and includes intellect, ideals, emotions, discernment, and decision. Tertullian, an early Christian writer from Carthage, North Africa, summarizes, "Without the soul, we are nothing. There is not even the name of a human being—only that of a carcass."[3] C. I. Scofield writes "The soul is the seat of the affections, desires, emotions, and the will of man (Mt. 11:29, 26:38; Jn. 12:27)."[4] The three main components of the soul are the mind, the emotions, and the will.

Several early church theologians wrote of their insights into our human existence. Although Tertullian did not view the spirit of man as a separate faculty from the human soul, his writings concerning the soul are insightful:

> The attributes that belong to the soul's own proper condition are these: immortality, rationality, sensibility, in-

telligence, and freedom of the will....I indeed maintain that both [body and soul] are conceived and formed perfectly simultaneously. They are also born together. Not a moment's interval occurs in their conception. Therefore, neither one can be assigned a prior place.[5]

Origen, a pupil of Clement and a prolific writer of the pre-Nicene church, wrote, "That the human soul lives and subsists after its separation from the body is believed not only among Christians and Jews, but also by many others among the Greeks [such as Plato] and barbarians." Methodius, a fourth century bishop from Lycia, wrote: "It is the body that dies; the soul is immortal."[6]

The Spirit

The most inward dimension of our being is called "spirit." In the New Testament, the Greek word *pneuma* is translated "spirit." Like its Old Testament counterpart *ruwach*, the Greek root meaning of "spirit" refers to "wind," "breath," or "force." Thus both the Hebrew and Greek languages refer to the "spirit" as the energizing life-force, the innermost spiritual part of our existence (1 Cor. 2:11).

The "spirit" of man, which is indeed conscience of God (Job. 32:8; Ps. 18:28; Eccl. 12:7; Prov. 20:27), includes an "intuition" component, which senses independently from outside influence, (Matt. 26:41; Mk. 8:12; Jn. 11:33; Acts 18:5) and an ability to worship and to communicate with God when enabled by the Holy Spirit (Jn. 4:23-24; 1 Cor.14:2; Rom. 8:16, 26; 1 Cor. 14:15-16). The human spirit came directly from God (Num. 16:22) and must some day return to God (Eccl. 12:7).

Man "with Christ"

The acceptance of Jesus Christ as Lord and Savior is the only solution to restoring intimacy with God, which was lost in Eden. By the purchasing power of Christ's own blood a believing individual is completely (spirit, soul, and body) redeemed to God. *"For ye are bought with a price: therefore glorify God in your body, and in your spirit, which are God's"* (1 Cor. 6:20). Prior to this, the whole of man is spiritually dead (separated from God). Before spiritual rebirth, an individual's spirit is suppressed. As no spiritual fellowship with God exists the spirit only communicates matters of moral law (Rom. 2:15) and a yearning for the Creator to the soul.

In this unsaved state, the depraved tendencies of the flesh overwhelm the soul with lusting. The soul itself is prone to selfish and prideful bents. In this degenerate condition man has much to promote sin and little to affect godly conduct. As an unregenerate individual ages and physically matures, the functions of the mind, emotions, and the will grow stronger to the extent that the spirit has a diminishing effect. This is why most individuals who trust Christ as Savior do so as children, while the conscience and will are tender and pliable. With time our inner man becomes more stubborn and self-fixed.

The longer the soul of man is apart from God, the more difficult it is for him to submit to God's sole remedy for spiritual death. The Lord Jesus said, *"I am the Way, the Truth, and the Life; no man cometh unto the Father, but by Me"* (Jn. 14:6). Once Christ is embraced and regeneration has occurred, then *"The Spirit itself beareth witness with **our spirit**, that we are the children of God"* (Rom. 8:16) – active communication and communion with God is established. The power of the Holy Spirit is then *available* to overcome our inherent depravity.

> *For the law of the Spirit of life in Christ Jesus hath made me free from the law of sin and death* (Rom. 8:2).

> *Having therefore these promises, dearly beloved, let us cleanse ourselves from **all filthiness of the flesh and spirit**, perfecting holiness in the fear of God* (2 Cor. 7:1).

From a human perspective, we speak of these three qualities of consciousness in the order of their importance to our fallen state: body, soul, and spirit. But when a human being has become a new creation through the regeneration by the Holy Spirit, these aspects of consciousness are properly ordered for service: spirit, soul, and body (1 Thess. 5:23). From God's vantage point, we must deny the desires of our flesh and of self to be fitted for service (Lk. 9:23-24). The spiritual reality to *"seek first the kingdom of God and His righteousness"* (Matt. 6:33) is realized in our being, while our personal whims and base appetites lose their control over us.

Irenaeus, a second century bishop of the church at Lyons (in modern day France) wrote describing the pull upon the soul by the flesh and our spirit:

> The complete man is composed of flesh, soul, and spirit. One of these does indeed preserve and fashion [the man] – the spirit. It is united and formed to another – the flesh. Then there is that which is between these two – the soul.

The soul is sometimes indeed raised up by it, when it follows the spirit. But sometimes the soul sympathizes with the flesh and falls into carnal lusts.[1]

Although the believer is a new creation and has a new nature, the old nature has not been eradicated. The Apostle Paul affirms the warring of these two natures within the believer (Rom. 7). The battle zone is the soul or, more specifically, the mind. The Spirit of God speaking through man's spirit is in direct opposition to the lusts of the body and the soul.

> *For I know that in me (that is, in my flesh), dwelleth no good thing: for to will is present with me; but how to perform that which is good I find not* (Rom. 7:18).

Yes, God speaks, convicts, draws, and chastens us, but He does not force the believer to choose rightly. The decisions of behavior and conduct are left to us – who will we listen to and obey? Thus, every believer has the opportunity to show love to the Savior by freely offering himself or herself as a living sacrifice to the Lord (Rom. 12:1-2). When the believer says "no" to the flesh and "yes" to his or her spirit, a sweet aroma ascends up into the nostrils of God for His enjoyment and refreshment.

> The soul is the place where man's supreme and final battles are fought.
>
> Abraham Neuman

> Physical life is given and maintained by God (Matt. 6:25-34). Meaningful and fulfilled life comes only when it is free to give itself to God as a disciple of Jesus Christ.
>
> Christian Wolf

When the Lord saves a repentant sinner, He completely re-deems that person's spirit, soul, and body. The soul and the spirit are immediately delivered from the penalty of sin when one confesses his sinfulness before God and accepts Christ's free gift of salvation (Jn. 5:24). The body practically realizes salvation when it is raptured from the presence of sin, after a complete overhaul called glorification. This transformation will occur for all living believers (simultaneously) at the coming of the Lord Jesus for His church (1 Thess. 4:13-17). In a twinkling of an eye, what was corruptible will be incorruptible, and what was mortal will be immortal (1 Cor. 15:51-52). The believer's body will be instantly transformed: sin and pain will cease to exist in it. The believer's glorified body will be enabled to worship and to please God without any hindrances of the flesh or ills of its previously fallen state. In summary, an individual's soul and spirit are eternally saved when he or she trusts the gospel message, while salvation of the body is to be greatly anticipated in a coming day. This was Paul's blessed hope (Tit. 2:13) and his earnest expectation *"...now is our salvation nearer than when we believed"* (Rom. 13:11).

God's offer for salvation is a complete salvation of the whole of man through Jesus Christ! The spirit is saved (Acts 7:59; 1 Cor. 6:20; 1 Cor. 5:5), the soul is saved (Jam. 5:20; Matt. 10:28), and the body will be saved (Phil. 3:21; 1 Cor. 15:51-52). It is through Christ that man's deepest need is satisfied. In Christ we are significant, for we are one with Him; we are both needed and wanted. In Christ we find security, for we are eternally safe and all our needs are provided for as He sees fit. We have God's assurance that if we die before the saving of the body (at the rapture of the church), we, that is our spiritual essence, will be in His presence (Rev. 6:9). "We are confident, I say, and willing rather to be absent from the body, and to be present with the Lord" (2 Cor. 5:8).

Through the finished work of Jesus Christ, the damage done by man through sin is repaired. Man is reconciled to his Creator. In fact, the believer has far more in Christ than Adam enjoyed in Garden of Eden. Adam was not justified (declared righteous) in Christ or indwelt by the Holy Spirit. Adam was not told that he would rule and reign with Christ (1 Cor. 4:8; 2 Tim. 2:12) or inherit all things with Christ (Rom. 8:17). But the believer's identification and spiritual union with Christ ensures these realities. It is just like God to miraculously build upon man's failures in such a way as to convey a wider blessing to the very creature that caused Him the most pain.

A Perfect Heart and a Willing Mind

We have observed from Scripture that we exist in a three-fold composition of spirit, soul, and body. The consequences of sin intruding into humanity adversely affected our entire being. God's remedy for man's physical, emotional, and spiritual difficulties is found in Jesus Christ. In Christ we have eternal life, but Christ-likeness comes through the sanctifying work of the Holy Spirit – it is a life long process. In Christ, our relationship with God is secure; it is based on what God has done by grace. However, maintaining communion and fellowship is based on our conduct, not God's. We are as close to the Lord right now as we want to be. The Lord is no respecter of persons – He has no favorites, just intimates. For the purpose of pursuing Christ-likeness we must explore more deeply into the soul of man.

Scripture rightly divides spirit, soul, and body, and then provides a further distinction within the human soul of the "heart" and "mind." As with soul and spirit, the Greek language conveys a more noticeable contrast between heart and mind than observed in Hebrew.

> *And thou, Solomon my son, know thou the God of thy father, and **serve him with a perfect heart and with a willing mind:** for the LORD searcheth all hearts, and understandeth all the imaginations of the thoughts: if thou seek him, he will be found of thee; but if thou forsake him, he will cast thee off forever* (1 Chr. 28:9).

*But when **his heart was lifted up, and his mind hardened in pride**, he was deposed from his kingly throne, and they took his glory from him* (Dan. 5:20).

*And the peace of God, which passeth all understanding, shall keep **your hearts and minds** through Christ Jesus* (Phil. 4:7).

*For this is the covenant that I will make with the house of Israel after those days, saith the Lord; **I will put my laws into their mind, and write them in their hearts**: and I will be to them a God, and they shall be to me a people* (Heb. 8:10).

The distinction of heart and mind is also a reality God acknowledges in His own eternal being.

*And **I will raise me up a faithful priest, that shall do according to that which is in mine heart and in my mind**: and I will build him a sure house; and he shall walk before mine anointed for ever* (1 Sam. 2:35).

*Then said the LORD unto me, Though Moses and Samuel stood before me, **yet my mind** could not be toward this people: cast them out of my sight, and let them go forth* (Jer. 15:1).

*And it repented the LORD that he had made man on the earth, and **it grieved him at his heart*** (Gen. 6:6).

*And the LORD smelled a sweet savour; and **the LORD said in his heart**, I will not again curse the ground any more for man's sake; for the imagination of man's heart is evil from his youth ...* (Gen. 8:21).

Tertullian correctly observed that the New Testament writers focused their instruction on the particulars of the soul rather than upon the soul itself. He writes, "As for 'the man within,' indeed, the apostle prefers its being regarded as the mind and heart rather than the soul."[1] The Old Testament writers certainly refer to the heart and mind, but the Hebrew language is more limited in expressing the same level of distinction as the Greek.

The Hebrew word *leb* and its synonym *lebab* appear 860 times in the Old Testament and are generally translated as "heart." However, ten times *leb* is rendered "mind." While *leb* is applied in various ways to convey different meanings, in the context of our subject the word focuses on inner feelings, emotions, inclinations, and moral character. The Hebrew word translated "mind" in the above verses is *nephesh*, which defines the mental vitality of a living soul. Thus, *nephesh* is generally translated "soul," but in some passages "heart." However, when both the "heart" and "mind" are spoken of in a compound manner, as in 1 Samuel 2:35, the distinction of these two Hebrew words, though mild, is observed.

The Lord Jesus acknowledged the essence of human constitution when declaring the most important commandment to be obeyed:

> *And thou shalt love the Lord thy God with all **thy heart**, and with all **thy soul**, and with all **thy mind**, and with all **thy strength**: this is the first commandment* (Mk. 12:30).

Commenting on this verse, William MacDonald states:

> This means that man's first obligation is to love God with the totality of his being. ... the heart speaks of the emotional nature, the soul of the volitional [self choos-

ing] nature, the mind of the intellectual nature, and the strength of the physical nature.[2]

John D. Grassmick similarly concludes:

... the various terms relating to the human personality – heart (control center; cf. Mark 7:19), soul (self-conscience life; cf. 8:35-36), mind (thought capacity), and strength (bodily powers).[3]

The Mind

So not to overwhelm some readers with human physiology, the scriptural analysis of the mind and heart are contained in the Appendix. For those readers desiring more than a summary description of the heart and mind, please consult the Appendix.

The Hebrew and Greek languages possess no word that is parallel to the English word *mind*. As a result, the Old Testament employs six different Hebrew terms to express aspects of man's intellectual activity and ability, while the New Testament imposes six nouns and five verbs to express different attributes of one's cognitive powers. The Greek language provides more clarity in defining the difference between the "mind" and "heart" than does the Hebrew. From the Greek language the following is derived as the meaning of the mind – "the seat of reflective consciousness, comprising the faculties of perception and understanding, and the ability to reason with rational thought."

The Heart

What does the "heart" of man refer to in the Bible? Certainly the heart organ may be referred to, but more generally the "heart" refers to an invisible component of the human soul relating to emotions, desires, moral inclinations and cognitive abilities. Figuratively the heart is the hidden spring of the personal and inward life.

In summary, the Greek terms for "soul," "heart," and "mind" (as relating to man) are not generally interchangeable and in fact relate to deepening interdependent realms of self-consciousness. The soul expresses the entire personality, including the seat of the affections, desires, emotions, and the will of man. The "heart" would figuratively be the core of man's soul – the seat of moral character, emotions, the will, and reasoning abilities. The "mind" speaks of reflective consciousness at the center of the "heart" and includes the ability to perceive, understand, analyze, and determine (judge by rational thought). The mind of man would then be directly influenced by the deceitfulness and wickedness of the heart's depraved state (Jer. 17:9).

Picture a circular target with a bull's-eye in the center and an inner and outer ring surrounding the bull's-eye. The outer ring would represent the soul – all that self-conscious man is; the next inner ring would represent the heart – man's desires, character, reasoning capabilities, emotions and will; and the bull's-eye would picture the mind – only man's cognitive abilities. When one refers to the soul, the mind and heart are included. When speaking of the heart, the mind is included. The following illustration depicts these centric relationships within the soul, as pertinent to the focused attack upon the mind. The figure is not meant to be a full model of the soul.[4]

The Battleground of the Soul – the Mind
Figure 1

Let us again review David's admonition to Solomon, *"... know thou the God of thy father, **and serve Him with a perfect heart and with a willing mind**: for the LORD **searcheth all hearts, and understandeth all the imaginations of the thoughts**: if thou seek Him, He will be found of thee; but if thou forsake Him, He will cast thee off forever"* (1 Chr. 28:9). David instructed Solomon to serve with a pure heart (speaking of integrity of motive) and with a mind that intellectually and rationally sought the Lord. It is possible for the heart to have a firm moral foundation, but if the mind succumbs to temptation the whole body suffers. Is it any wonder then that the mind is prone to satanic assault? The mind is not our innermost being, but it is the bull's-eye of our total being when it comes to behavior. To be Christ-like, a believer must command his mind according to the appeals of his spirit to control the whole person. The Holy Spirit is available and willing to respond to aid the believer to achieve this endeavor, as he or she willfully submits to the rule of his or her own spirit.

> *And every man that striveth for the mastery is temperate in all things. Now they do it to obtain a corruptible crown; but we an incorruptible. I therefore so run, not as uncertainly; so fight I, not as one that beateth the air: But **I keep under my body, and bring it into subjection:** lest that by any means, when I have preached to others, I myself should be a castaway* (1 Cor. 9:25-27).

Proper control of the mind is absolutely necessary to the pursuit of Christ-likeness and fruit bearing. If the mind is depressed, spiritual control of the body is diminished. Reinforce the mind unto righteousness, and the heart will be molded and guarded. Consequently, Scripture in general, does not exhort the heart to action, but the mind. The heart responds with faith, love, hope, joy, etc., as it has been conditioned by the mind. If the mind allows the flesh nature to control the heart, the whole body will be adversely affected. Selfish desires and ambitions become more rooted in the heart as unrestrained behavior continues. But if the mind is attentive to the spirit, the heart will be prone to godly emotions and actions.

Mental slavery is mental death, and every man who has given up his intellectual freedom is the living coffin of his dead soul.

Robert Green Ingersoll

Though the soul is the life of man and has tremendous capabilities, it, nevertheless, cannot accomplish the task of fruit bearing without the power of the Holy Spirit. As the Holy Spirit gains more and more access of the whole body, the believer produces "fruit," and then "more fruit," and then "much fruit" (Jn. 15:1-5). Consequently, all the talent, intellect, knowledge, wisdom, and natural abilities that the soul might boast are completely unable to generate spiritual blessing. These must all be brought under the command of the spirit as controlled by the Holy Spirit.

"I Know Your Thoughts"

How much of our mind and thought life does God really know? As our Creator, it is obvious that He knows us better than we know ourselves. He not only foreknows our lifespan, failures, and how we will react to a particular situation in advance, but He also knows our thoughts before their mental conception and our words before our lips form speech. His penetrating insight into our whole person dazzles the mind with awe, and yet promotes an eerie sense of nakedness before our Creator.

> And the Spirit of the LORD fell upon me, and said unto me, Speak; Thus saith the LORD; Thus have ye said, O house of Israel: for **I know the things that come into your mind**, every one of them (Ezek. 11:5).

> O Lord, Thou hast searched me, and known me. Thou knowest my downsitting and mine uprising; **Thou understandest my thought afar off.** Thou compassest my path and my lying down, and **art acquainted with all my ways**. For there is not a word in my tongue, but, lo, O Lord, Thou knowest it altogether (Ps. 139:1-4).

> I know that thou canst do every thing, and that no thought can be withholden from thee (Job 42:2).

Ponder for a moment that darkest secret that you try to keep hidden from everyone else. Yes, the Lord knows all about it. What about that thought bent that continues to plague your mind – the one you just cannot seem to overcome. He knows all about that, too. What you are thinking presently as you read this sentence. Yes, He knew your thoughts before you were born. Time does not imprison God as it does us. Time was created as part of creation; before creation, time was meaningless (2 Tim. 1:9, NIV). How else will the sins of lustful imaginations be judged if God does not know our thoughts (Matt. 5:28)?

God intimately knows our minds, and He also has a righteous desire for each of our minds. The following verses indicate God's desire for the believer's mind, namely that the mind be settled, sound, and spiritual.

> ***That ye be not soon shaken in mind***, *or be troubled, neither by spirit, nor by word, nor by letter as from us, as that the day of Christ is at hand* (2 Thess. 2:2).

> *For God hath not given us the spirit of fear; but of power, and of love, and of **a sound mind*** (2 Tim. 1:7).

> *Among whom also we all had our conversation in times past in the lusts of our flesh, **fulfilling the desires of the flesh and of the mind**; and were by nature the children of wrath, even as others* (Eph. 2:3).

> *For to be **carnally minded is death***; *but to **be spiritually minded is life and peace**. Because the carnal mind is enmity against God: for it is not subject to the law of God, neither indeed can be. So then they that are in the flesh cannot please God. But ye are not in the flesh, but in the Spirit, if so be that the Spirit of God dwell in you. Now if any man have not the Spirit of Christ, he is none of His* (Rom. 8:6-9).

The believer's mind is to be spiritual and sound – not self-desiring or easily shaken. An overly active or anxious mind will affect and disturb the quietness of the spirit. If the spirit is not clearly heard, emotions or high-speed thinking may confuse proper guidance through the Holy Spirit, the result of which is independent action in opposition to God.

> To the quiet mind all things are possible. What is the quiet mind? A quiet mind is one that nothing weighs on, nothing worries, which, free from ties and from all self-seeking, is wholly merged into the will of God and dead to its own.

> Meister Eckhart

If the mind is settled, the direction of the spirit is clearly understood and spiritual reasoning prevails to align the will and the heart Godward. Thus, Scripture generally exhorts the believer's mind to action and not his heart, for the heart will respond as the mind has allowed it to be conditioned by the desires of the flesh or of the spirit. Who or what rules the mind will also rule the heart, though the heart responds beyond the mind's capability! This is why faith, love, giving, rejoicing, etc. are related to the heart and not the mind. These are not intellectual matters.

> *Therefore did **my heart rejoice**, and my tongue was glad; moreover also my flesh shall rest in hope* (Acts 2:26).

> *Ye stiffnecked and **uncircumcised in heart** and ears, ye do always **resist** the Holy Ghost: as your fathers did, so do ye* (Acts 7:51).

> *But after thy **hardness and impenitent heart** treasurest up unto thyself wrath against the day of wrath and revelation of the righteous judgment of God* (Rom. 2:5).

> *That if thou shalt confess with thy mouth the Lord Jesus,
> and shalt **believe in thine heart** that God hath raised
> Him from the dead, thou shalt be saved. For with the
> heart man believeth unto righteousness; and with the
> mouth confession is made unto salvation* (Rom. 10:9-10).

> *Every man according as **he purposeth in his heart, so let
> him give**; not grudgingly, or of necessity: for God loveth
> a cheerful giver* (2 Cor. 9:7).

> *Speaking to yourselves in psalms and hymns and spiri-
> tual songs, singing and **making melody in your heart** to
> the Lord* (Eph. 5:19).

> *Now the end of the commandment is **charity out of a
> pure heart**, and of a good conscience, and of faith un-
> feigned* (1 Tim. 1:5).

The mind cannot rationalize the operation of faith (a living trust in an unseen God that cannot be confirmed through the senses). "Now faith is the substance of things hoped for, the evidence of things not seen" (Heb. 11:1). The world says, "Show me and I will believe" (see Jn. 6:30), but the spiritual man proclaims, "By believing I see and understand" (see Jn. 6:69). When God has demonstrated His presence through signs and wonders, these have proven insufficient to cause the unrighteous to repent or to significantly build up the faith of the righteous. Israel's faith was not increased during their desert excursion, though they visibly witnessed the Lord's goodness to them daily. Egypt did not repent after being judged ten times by divine plagues, each of which targeted a pagan god to demonstrate Jehovah's supremacy. Israel failed to repent during the miracle-saturated prophetic ministries of Elijah and Elisha. While Christ walked upon the earth the general Jewish population viewed His numerous miracles with contempt or as thrilling entertainment, but rejected His message. Faith is not an intellectual matter; it is an exercise of the heart.

This is not to say that the mind is not engaged in rendering a decision to trust Christ for salvation, for indeed God has revealed much evidence of Himself through creation, conscience, changed lives, miracles, and His Word. The mind logically evaluates these evidences of truth, but the pull of the spirit upon the heart, as provided through the conviction of the Holy Spirit, will be required to exercise faith. Faith cannot be verified by the senses or rationalized by the mind. It is as if God is saying, "I have shown you all this evidence of My handiwork. Now will you trust Me with your soul based solely on what I say?" The last step to receive salvation is one of faith – intellectualism will not bridge the gap between what can be affirmed and what must be by faith.

When God declared His covenant with Abraham, his wife Sarah was past the childbearing stage of life, and the couple had no children. Rationally speaking, there was no chance of Abraham becoming the natural father of many nations. But how did Abraham respond when God declared this promise to him? *"And he believed in the LORD; and He counted it to him for righteousness"* (Gen. 15:6). Abraham trusted God, even though he had no idea of how He was going to keep His promise. Faith is a heart matter, and God knew Abraham's heart!

The mind, which is at the center of the heart, cannot rationalize giving without receiving something or having joy in promises yet unseen. The heart acts upon the mind from its developed or undeveloped moral character, emotions, and the soul's inherent self will. This is why Solomon directs his son to "keep" and "guard" his heart.

My son, forget not my law; but let thine heart keep my commandments (Prov. 3:1).

Keep thy heart with all diligence; for out of it are the issues of life (Prov. 4:23).

We are to guard against allowing an erosion of moral virtue in the heart. The heart is to be protected, and the mind is the protector. This is why scriptural exhortation is directed at the believer's mind. But if the mind does not keep the heart pure and undefiled, the heart gains an adverse influence upon the will. Once emotional responses are interjected into the will, the believer begins a slide downward into selfish ambition and carnal behavior. As a result, the internal wantonness of flesh and self overpower the intellectual reasoning of the mind. The mind is confused and prone to ignore the spirit's voice. When the enemy monitors carnal behavior, he moves in like a lion upon its helpless prey. Satan and his evil spirits bombard the believer's mind with suggestions in order to establish strongholds and strengthen immoral bents. What can we do to overcome this situation? Practically speaking, how do we strengthen our minds to guard our hearts? How do we successfully ward off satanic suggestions? How do we avoid being depressed by circumstances and from allowing our own imagination from getting the best of us?

Mental Fitness

Have you ever been confronted with one of those irritating charts that coordinates a person's height with their ideal weight? Many of us just ignore such agitating information and live the way we want to; that is, until some medical condition arises that awakens us to the reality that our dietary and exercise habits directly affect our overall body's health. Some recent estimates tie 70 to 90 percent of our health-related problems to our individual patterns of diet and exercise. The medical chart merely highlighted where we should be, but the matter of remaining at that ideal body weight is nothing more than personal discipline, barring some constraining medical condition. Let us boldly face the facts: most of us are overweight because we choose to be. We do not exercise as we ought, and we thumb our noses at nutritious foods. This lethargic attitude to fitness degrades the mind also. If we want healthy functioning minds, we must both exercise and feed the mind properly.

The ideal operation and performance of the mind was shown in the last chapter. How did you measure up? Do you have a sound mind that is not prone to be easily shaken or think of self? If not, the following is a "fitness program" sure to strengthen your mind and benefit your mental health.

Mental Diet

The mind is strengthened in the same way that the muscles of our body are – through exercise and proper diet. Concerning appropriate diet, the Apostle Paul developed a wholesome dietary menu that is sure to enhance the vitality of the believer's thought life.

> *Finally, brethren, whatsoever things are true, whatsoever things are honest, whatsoever things are just, whatsoever things are pure, whatsoever things are lovely, whatsoever things are of good report; if there be any virtue, and if there be any praise, think on these things* (Phil. 4:8).

If the believer is going to expose his mind to violence, pornography, filthy language, course jesting, and extravagant indulgences, the heart will readily be conformed into a stagnant cesspool of carnal ambitions. *"For as he thinketh in his heart, so is he"* (Prov. 23:7). Physically you are what you eat, but spiritually you become what you think upon. It is simply the sowing and reaping principles of the harvest. The three laws of the harvest are: (1) you reap what you sow; (2) you reap more than what you sow; and (3) you reap later than you sow. Paul explains that if *"a man soweth to his flesh, he shall of the flesh reap corruption"* (see Gal. 6:7-8). When a believer feeds on (thinks upon) what is corrupt, it must lead to a legitimate harvest of corruption. It will be realized long after the initial seeds were sown that the repercussions were far more devastating than what could have ever been imagined. The nude images that a young man tucks away in his mind will be used by Satan to stir up dissatisfaction with his own wife for many years to come. So why hurt yourself, your wife, your family, and your God? The harvest of pain is just not worth it. *"Flee also youth-*

*ful lusts, but follow righteousness, faith, love, peace, with them that **call on the Lord out of a pure heart**"* (2 Tim. 2:22).

The overall diet of the believer's mind boils down to proper thinking and discernment. Concerning appropriate discernment, Paul writes the following:

> *For your obedience is come abroad unto all men. I am glad therefore on your behalf: but yet I would **have you wise unto that which is good, and simple concerning evil**. And the God of peace shall bruise Satan under your feet shortly. The grace of our Lord Jesus Christ be with you. Amen* (Rom. 16:19-20).

The child of God is to discern between what is holy and what is evil, what is wise and what is foolish. What is holy and wise should be obeyed, and what is evil and foolish should be shunned. The matter of discerning between right and wrong behavior is dependent upon knowing the commandments of Scripture. Discerning between what is wise and what is foolish is dependent upon knowing God's commandments, warnings, principles, promises, and the lessons learned from personal narratives in Scripture. In fact, the Lord addressed the matter of being wise and not foolish much more often than the matter of what is right and what is wrong, though the latter would be included in what is wise and foolish. Gaining discernment of what is wise and what is foolish requires prayer, study, godly counsel, and the leading of the Holy Spirit in our lives.

As a believer relies on God's grace to accomplish holy living, the victory is won through Christ, and the devices of Satan are spoiled. The book of Joshua portrays this accomplishment in the narrative. The Israelites had soundly defeated the armies of the five southern Canaanite kings. The five kings themselves fled the battle to hide in a cave at Makkedah. The Israelites sealed the cave until Joshua arrived. Joshua is a strong Old Testament type of Christ; in fact, his name is identical to that of Jesus, "Jehovah saves." When Joshua arrived at the cave, he commanded the five kings to be brought out. He then addressed his captains:

> *Come near, put your feet upon the necks of these kings. And they came near, and put their feet upon the necks of them. And Joshua said unto them, Fear not, nor be dismayed, be strong and of good courage: for thus shall the LORD do to all your enemies against whom ye fight* (Josh. 10:24-25).

Afterwards Joshua slew all five kings himself. What is the significance of pressing one's foot on the neck of the enemy? God was allowing His children to share in the victory that was only possible through Him. It was not the captains that ultimately defeated the enemy, but Joshua, representing Christ.

Likewise, the Lord Jesus, speaking of His work at Calvary, claimed, *"Now is the judgment of this world; now shall the prince of this world be cast out. And I, if I be lifted up from the earth* [speaking of crucifixion, v. 33], *will draw all men unto Me"* (Jn. 12:31-32). Calvary was the prophetic fulfillment of Genesis 3:15. God speaking to the Serpent (Satan) *"And I will put enmity between thee and the woman, and between thy seed and her seed* [Christ]; *it* [Christ] *shall bruise thy* [Satan's] *head, and thou shalt bruise his* [Christ's] *heel."* The head of Satan was crushed at Calvary by the foot of the Lord Jesus. Consequently, the believer has ultimate victory in Christ over Satan. We are thus able to proclaim this victory in the present life as we rely on Christ's grace and live a simple existence, which loathes evil in thought and deed. The more "stuff" we accumulate, and the more we dabble in the world; the more opportunity we allow Satan to entangle our hearts and minds. He is more than happy to spiritually strangle us with our own idolatry of luxurious things. Dear Christian, think upon Philippians 4:8 and be discerning as described in Romans 16:19-20, and the Lord Jesus will bruise Satan under your feet.

> If a man lets his garden alone, it very soon ceases to be a
> garden; and if a saint lets his mind alone, it will soon become
> a rubbish heap for Satan to make use of.
>
> Oswald Chambers

Mental Exercises

No particular exercise strengthens all the muscles of the body; different exercises are required to maintain complete muscular fitness. The "bench press" does not strengthen the quadriceps, and "curls" ignore the hamstrings. Likewise, Scripture provides different strengthening exercises for mental fitness. Each exercise challenges a specific mental temperament by replacing an inappropriate bent with a godly thought pattern.

Our minds are such that we must think upon something. Not thinking upon something just doesn't work! For the next ten seconds (after reading this sentence) try clearing your mind of all thoughts and especially don't think about the letter "**R**" in the word "**R**ascal." So how did you do? It is very difficult not to think about something once it has been introduced into your mind. However, if you replace what you want to mentally escape with another thought, you can avoid this enigma. Sir Thomas More put it this way, "Occupy your mind with good thoughts, or the enemy will fill it with bad ones: unoccupied it cannot be."

Since our minds must ponder something, let us muse upon Christ and appropriate things, such as Scripture, hymns and spiritual songs. A Christian, who recently spent several months in a Chinese labor camp, highlighted the fact that meditating upon hymns of the faith helped him maintain hope in the midst of horrible conditions. We must think rightly and use biblical exercises to increase the mind's adherence to proper thinking.

Cults and New Age religions understand the fact that our minds must have something to think upon. Their agenda is to enlist unsuspecting recruits who will empty their minds to allow satanic dominion. Texe Marrs, the author of *New Age Cults and Religions*, lists control methods used by Eastern religions and cults, then provides this summary statement, "It is plain from reviewing the above list of tactics and techniques that mind control is a paramount goal of the cults. The person's mind must be attacked so that he or she comes under the effective control of either the cult leader or the cult group."[1] Texe Marrs acknowledges that one of the techniques applied to an emptied mind is hypnosis. "They induce a form of hypnosis in disciples, a state of altered consciousness or high suggestibility, through use of such techniques and exercises as vain repetitions or chanting, meditation, and visualization on mandalas or other occultic symbols."[2]

The Eastern form is to empty and then control the mind, while the Christian form is to fill the mind with thoughts of Christ! The following are six mind exercises to aid the believer to maintain a Christ focus.

Settling the Mind

How do you first react when there is distressing news? Do you think positively about it? Is your initial recourse to ponder how God might derive glory in the circumstance? He will, you know (Rom. 8:28). During the labor and delivery of our children, my wife focused on a small stuffed animal and practiced breathing exercises. The focusing of the mind on a visible object and the breathing exercises did nothing to diminish the travail of childbearing, but it did keep her mind preoccupied so as not to concentrate on the pain. Spiritually speaking, it requires practice and determination to refocus the mind on something lovely instead of what is causing the soul anxiety.

The prophet Samuel told Saul, who had been looking for his lost donkeys for three days, *"...set not thy mind on them; for they are found ..."* (1 Sam. 9:20). Clearly, it is possible to focus or set the mind on a particular thing by an act of the will. Isaiah informs us ultimately how to maintain peace in our minds, *"Thou wilt keep him in perfect peace, whose **mind is stayed on Thee [the Lord]**: because he trusteth in Thee* (Isa. 26:3).

The challenge in any fearful disaster or sorrowful event is to maintain an unruffled mind. A woman said to evangelist D. L. Moody, "I have found a promise that helps me when I am afraid. It is Psalm 56:3 – 'What time I am afraid, I will trust in Thee.'" Mr. Moody replied, "I have a better promise than that! Isaiah 12:2 – 'I will trust and not be afraid.'"[3] Certainly, both promises are true and each has its own application, but the latter speaks of a settled mind without the distraction of fear. This mind focus has immediate and complete trust of our helper the Lord Jesus Christ in unsettling times. Hudson Taylor once wrote from the China Sea concerning the Isaiah 12:2 promise, "Soon we shall be in the midst of the battle, but the Lord our God in the midst of us is mighty, so we 'will trust, and not be afraid' (Isa. 12:2)."[4]

On October 8-10, 1871, the city of Chicago was devastated by an inferno that destroyed 18,000 buildings and left 100,000 people homeless. All the principal hotels, public buildings, warehouses, grain elevators, steamboats, bridges, and railway stations were burnt. The total loss was estimated at $200,000,000 – a staggering fortune by 1871 dollars. The disaster left fifty-seven insurance companies insolvent, and plunged countless businesses and people into bankruptcy. Much of the physical kingdom that Dwight Moody had labored to build lay in ruins also. The Illinois Street Church, the second Farwell Hall, their gift house on State Street, and the Moody's home were all gone.[5]

After the fire had burned out, Moody went back to survey the ruins of his house. A friend came by and said to Moody, "I hear you lost everything." "Well," said Moody, "you understood wrong. I have a good deal more left than I lost." "What do you mean?" the inquisitive friend asked. "I didn't know you were that rich." Moody then opened his Bible (one of the few possessions he was able to save from his home), and read to him Revelation 21:7 – "He that overcometh shall inherit all things, and I will be his God."[6] Moody had the eternal focus despite overwhelming disappointment and a difficult future. However, he would later note that this event brought him into a higher plain of spiritual life that he had not known before. God brought a great blessing to Moody, which could not have been realized without the pain of being brought to the end of self.

Practice refocusing your mind on one thing and then another, while not letting the previous matter sneak back into primary contemplation. In the same way, the next time your mind becomes anxious, practice inviting Christ into your thought-life. Allow the Lord Jesus to be the focus of your attention. Let your mind ponder potential divine solutions or outcomes to the situation by which the Lord will glorify Himself. This will settle your mind. The mind must have something to focus on – who better than the Lord?

Recalling to Mind

The exercise of "recalling" is similar to that of "settling," but requires the mind to focus backwards into its own memory in lieu of potential future divine solutions. In this mental exercise, one recalls either the past faithfulness of God or His promises and directives. We are creatures that tend to forget the Lord, our past mistakes, and His past faithfulness. Thus, there is much exhortation in Scripture to remember the Lord, His goodness and His commands (Deut. 6:12, 8:11, 9:7; Lk. 22:19). The prophet Isaiah instructed God's people to recall: *"Remember this, and show yourselves men: bring it again to mind, O ye transgressors. Remember the former things of old: for I am God, and there is none else; I am God, and there is none like Me"* (Isa. 46:8-9).

What is the benefit of refocusing the mind backward upon historical events or divine statements? We reacquaint ourselves with God's promises of deliverance and recall His past faithfulness through the storms of life.

> *There hath no temptation taken you but such as is common to man: but God is faithful, who will not suffer you to be tempted above that ye are able; but will with the temptation **also make a way to escape, that ye may be able to bear it*** (1 Cor. 10:13).

> *Let your conversation be without covetousness; and be content with such things as ye have: for He hath said, **I will never leave thee, nor forsake thee**. So that we may boldly say, The Lord is my helper, and I will not fear what man shall do unto me* (Heb. 13:5-6).

As the mind processes the information, a sense of hope infuses our soul – He guided us through perilous times before, and He has promised to do it again. The heart is again stirred up to have faith and trust. The prophet Jeremiah wrote the following shortly after the decimation of Jerusalem by Babylonian invaders:

> This *I recall to my mind, therefore have I hope*. *It is of the LORD's mercies that we are not consumed, because His compassions fail not. They are new every morning: great is Thy faithfulness. **The LORD is my portion, saith my soul; therefore will I hope in Him***. *The LORD is good unto them that wait for Him, to the soul that seeketh Him. It is good that a man should both hope and quietly wait for the salvation of the LORD* (Lam. 3:21-26).

The author and his wife are commended workers who serve the Lord full time without any commitments of salary or without solicitations for money. It is a wonderful way to live as we are constantly casting ourselves before the Lord with specific financial needs. Year after year the Lord has provided for all of our needs and even some of our wants. Our faith grows through each trial, and it is an increasingly delightful experience just to call upon the name of the Lord and experience His manifold blessings. We have a very rich Father! There are perhaps a hundred stories the author could share, but one particular provision in the early days of our great adventure of faith comes to mind first.

On a Saturday, in April 1999, we paid a local garage $360 plus pocket change to repair our 1991 S-10 truck. We paid the expense via a credit card, then prayed to the Lord for His portion. Following our convictions, we informed no one else about the matter. The next day, Sunday, we received an anonymous gift from someone in our assembly for $100. In Monday's mail, we received another $100 gift from a small church in Kansas, and then in Tuesday's mail we received a third $100 gift of fellowship from a couple in Wisconsin. My wife and I praised the

Lord for His provision, knowing we could handle the outstanding $60 on our own to pay off the debt. Later that day I traveled to a home-schooling program in which I taught two Bible classes. After the last class, one of the students, a teenage girl, greeted me with a silent smile and handed me a card before departing from the classroom. I opened the card and found a lovely note of appreciation for the class and three $20 bills. A ten dollar bill would have been much appreciated, but the fact that it was $60 reaffirmed in my mind that the Lord had specifically "fully" answered our prayers in only three days concerning the truck repair expenses. It is noteworthy that the two letters received (with $100 checks) were mailed prior to our need being known to us and that the one couple had never before financially fellowshipped with us. This was all God's doing, and He was not going to share the glory of the matter with us. He faithfully answered our prayers. To Him be all the glory!

"But my God shall supply all your need according to His riches in glory by Christ Jesus. Now unto God and our Father be glory for ever and ever. Amen" (Phil. 4:19-20). When trials come, recall God's past goodness; it will secure your mind, and grow your faith!

Renewing the mind

So far we have learned to shift our thinking from present circumstances to ponder how the Lord might use the situation for His glory or to His past faithfulness and declared promises. "Renewing" is a third way of refocusing the mind. Renewing relinquishes carnal and worldly thinking to meditate upon the acceptable will of God.

I beseech you therefore, brethren, by the mercies of God, that ye present your bodies a living sacrifice, holy, ac-

ceptable unto God, which is your reasonable service. And be not conformed to this world: **but be ye transformed by the renewing of your mind,** *that ye may prove what is that good, and acceptable, and perfect, will of God* (Rom. 12:2).

And **be renewed in the spirit of your mind** (Eph. 4:23).

Perhaps you have heard a Christian pray for the Lord to show him or her His will for their life on a particular matter. Actually, as far as the believer is concerned, the will of God is known for their lives. What is really needed is daily guidance. God's will for the life of every believer is known, though His plan for each individual is quite varied and beautiful. The question is, "Do you want to do the will of God?" Note the following verses that clearly state what the will of God is for your life.

Servants, be obedient to them that are your masters according to the flesh, with fear and trembling, in singleness of your heart, as unto Christ; not with eyeservice, as menpleasers; but as the servants of Christ, **doing the will of God from the heart;** *with good will doing service, as to the Lord, and not to men: knowing that whatsoever good thing any man doeth, the same shall he receive of the Lord, whether he be bond or free* (Eph. 6:5-8).

For this is the will of God, *even your sanctification, that ye should abstain from fornication* (1 Thess. 4:3).

In every thing give thanks: **for this is the will of God** *in Christ Jesus concerning you* (1 Thess. 5:18).

For so is the will of God, *that with well doing ye may put to silence the ignorance of foolish men* (1 Pet. 2:15).

> *Love not the world, neither the things that are in the world. If any man love the world, the love of the Father is not in him. For all that is in the world, the lust of the flesh, and the lust of the eyes, and the pride of life, is not of the Father, but is of the world. And the world passeth away, and the lust thereof:* **but he that doeth the will of God** *abideth for ever* (1 Jn. 2:15-17).

As a believer renews his mind (thinks upon what is the good and perfect will of God), he or she is transformed from carnal thinking to holy living. This technique of strengthening the mind will be found helpful for those that are prone to think selfishly, to compare themselves with others, or to have proud thoughts. If one has dwelt on an inappropriate thought, he or she should confess it as sin; however, this action in and of itself will not overcome the mental bent. One must replace inappropriate thinking with proper thinking. So, for selfish thoughts refocus the mind on how self can serve for the glory of God instead of how I can be served. Remembering God's sovereignty in creation and His unique purpose for each of our lives will help replace "comparing" thoughts. Simply remembering that I can do nothing for God's pleasure naturally (Rom. 7:18, 8:8), but that *"I can do all things through Christ who strengthens me"* (Phil. 4:13) will aid in overcoming prideful thoughts. If godly thinking does not initially repel the thought, confess the ill imagination as sin, then seek to replace it with a holy inclination.

This is one of the most important mental exercises that a Christian can do. The flesh furnishes a base of operation for the enemy's evil intentions. When the believer does not renew his mind, he exposes a great deal of territory for the adversary to besiege and dig in. The enemy gains a stronghold.

The difference between worldliness and godliness is a renewed mind.

Erwin W. Lutzer

Persuading the Mind

This aspect of mind exercise forces vague thinking to specific reasoning. It brings blurred conduct into focus. Young Christians often have difficulties working out the *gray zone* areas of liberty. The Old Testament had hundreds of laws that could never be fully obeyed (Gal. 3:10-12). The purpose of the law was to show sin and to point the Jews to the solution – their Messiah Jesus Christ (Rom. 3:20; Gal. 3:24). In the New Testament, grace reigns on behalf of the believer; consequently, very few "dos and don'ts" are levied. God desires that love and not fear be the motive for service (1 Jn. 4:18). The Lord desires us to work out our salvation [sanctified living] with fear and trembling before Him. He desires us to be holy for He is holy (1 Pet. 1:16).

The task then is to reduce the gray zone area of liberty into appropriate personal conduct that neither offends one's conscience or the edicts of Scripture. The believer doesn't function in a fog of unclear notions, but becomes fully persuaded in his or her mind what is right and what is wrong behavior. This behavior glorifies God and does what is spiritually edifying for self and others; it does not stumble the lost or a weaker brother or make provision for the flesh to be master.

*One man esteemeth one day above another: another esteemeth every day alike. Let every **man be fully persuaded in his own mind** (Rom. 14:5).*

*Wherefore, my beloved, as ye have always obeyed, not as in my presence only, but now much more in my absence, **work out your own salvation with fear and trembling*** (Phil. 2:12).

*And he that doubteth is damned if he eat, because he eateth not of faith: **for whatsoever is not of faith is sin*** (Rom. 14:23).

*Whether therefore ye eat, or drink, or whatsoever ye do, do all to the glory of God. **Give no offence, neither to the Jews, nor to the Gentiles, nor to the church of God:** Even as I please all men in all things, not seeking mine own profit, but the profit of many, that they may be saved* (1 Cor. 10:31-33).

*All things are lawful unto me, but all things are not expedient: all things are lawful for me**, but I will not be brought under the power of any*** (1 Cor. 6:12).

*And **through thy knowledge [liberty] shall the weak brother perish**, for whom Christ died? But when ye sin so against the brethren, and wound their weak conscience, ye sin against Christ* (1 Cor. 8:11-12).

In today's indulgent culture, many Christians seem to think that if they remain ignorant of their sin, they are not sinning. Though they are not mindful of their sinful behavior, God is! D. L. Moody wrote in the front of his Bible, "This book will keep you from sin or sin will keep you from this book." There is nothing wrong with marking in your Bible, but dear reader is your Bible marking you? Explore the Bible. Let God's Word change you. Be fully persuaded of what is God-honoring conduct and what is not – don't live in self-imposed ignorance concerning holiness.

Holiness is not the end of progress, but deliverance from standing still.

G. Campbell Morgan

Not to decide is to decide.

Harvey Cox

Girding the Mind

Girding the mind relates to the exercise of focusing the mind on accomplishing an intended goal no matter what distractions, difficulties, and suffering is encountered. In ancient days, the hulls of ships were undergirded with ropes and cables to keep the hull from breaking apart in storms (Acts 27:17). The girding of the ship strengthened it for the strenuous time ahead. The marathon runner comprehends the cost that the race will impose on his body. He mentally prepares (girds his mind) for the forthcoming pain and the exhaustion that will soon beset him, then he runs with endurance to finish the race. He is not distracted by cramping muscles, blisters, shin splints, cottonmouth, etc. – he runs on for the prize; he runs to finish the race well.

> *Wherefore* **gird up the loins of your mind***, be sober, and* **hope to the end for the grace** *that is to be brought unto you at the revelation of Jesus Christ* (1 Pet. 1:13).

William MacDonald provides the following comments concerning this verse:

> Peter urges the saints to have a "girded" mind. The girding up of the mind is an interesting figure of speech. In

eastern lands, people wore long, flowing robes. When they wanted to walk fast or with a minimum of hindrance, they would tie the robe up around their waist with a belt (see Ex. 12:11). In this way they girded up their loins. But what does Peter mean by gird up the loins of your mind? As they went out into a hostile world, believers were to avoid panic and distraction. In times of persecution, there is always the tendency to become rattled and confused. A girded mind is one that is strong, composed, cool, and ready for action. It is unimpeded by distraction of human fear or persecution.[7]

If Christian in John Bunyan's *Pilgrims Progress* had girded his mind, he would have likely avoided the "slough of despond." Every devoted Christian is destined for trouble, but not for despair. *"Yea, and **all** that will live godly in Christ Jesus **shall** suffer persecution"* (2 Tim. 3:12). The Lord Jesus explained to His disciples, *"In the world you **shall have** tribulation: but be of good cheer; I have overcome the world"* (Jn. 16:33). Prepare your mind for the struggles ahead, and don't get bogged down in self-pity, grappling with despair when those forecasted storms of life arrive.

Readying the Mind

After a difficult workday or in the aftermath of a huge endeavor, there is a tendency for us to relax our minds. You know, just "zone out" for a bit, be a "couch potato." For a season at least, we just don't want to think about anything. This sluggard phenomenon is often accompanied by a craving for a bit of amusement (literally "a not thinking" activity); perhaps watching TV, or a movie, or listening to music. A ready mind is a mind that does not shut down, but remains focused, active, and available. Satan often does his most extensive programming through the portals of our soul (the eyes and ears) when we are fatigued. We listen to or view evil propaganda that we would not normally permit ourselves to digest. When our minds are shutdown, we cease to apply the Philippians 4:8 mental filter, and the filth just creeps in. There are times the believer should rest (Ps. 23:2), but the mind should remain sharp. Whenever we are conscious, our minds should be alert, available, and willing to serve when summoned by the Lord. The good soldier of the cross remains alert, for the enemy is cunning and lurks in unseen shadows for those who regrettably let their guard down.

*Feed the flock of God which is among you, taking the oversight thereof, not by constraint, but willingly; not for filthy lucre, **but of a ready mind** (1 Pet. 5:2).*

*For if there be first **a willing mind**, it is accepted according to that a man hath, and not according to that he hath not (2 Cor. 8:12).*

*And not that only, but who was also chosen of the churches to travel with us with this grace, which is administered by us to the glory of the same Lord, and **declaration of your ready mind** (2 Cor. 8:19).*

*But let us, who are of the day, **be sober**, putting on the breastplate of faith and love; and for an helmet, the hope of salvation (1 Thess. 5:8).*

Summary of Mental Exercises

Mental Exercise	Remove Focus From	New Mental Focus
Settling the Mind	Circumstances	How will God get the glory?
Recalling to Mind	Circumstances	The Lord's promises and past faithfulness.
Renewing the Mind	Carnal Thinking	The Lord's revealed will for godly behavior.
Persuading the Mind	Vague thinking	Specific thinking about godly conduct.
Girding the Mind	Suffering & Difficulties	The goal of the activity.
Readying the Mind	Inactivity	Active thinking.

It must be emphasized that these mental exercises are not for the purpose of increasing natural intellectual power (mind power) or to better serve God through natural strength and means. This would be foolish and only add to the tendency of the fallen soul to pursue God through soul abilities, especially if one is abundantly gifted. The intent of the above mind exercises is to settle and focus the mind, and to fortify it against carnal suggestion. This allows the soul to be more sensitive to the spirit's quiet voice.

If you have done any fishing, you know how difficult it is to see fish, even in clear water, when the wind churns up a lake. The waves and ripples reflect and bend light in such a way that the contour of submerged fish and their movements are undetectable. However, stillness allows the fisherman to spot fish nesting in the shallows or the slightest movement under the water. He responds instantly by casting the baited hook towards the intended target. In the same way, these scriptural exercises calm and focus the mind to better discern our spirit's voice.

Mind Frames

May these six exercises aid your mind to better focus upon spiritual matters and allow the Lord Jesus to more fully reside in your thoughts.

The Mental Battlefield

"Can Satan plant wicked thoughts in the minds of believers?" asked a dear sister in our assembly. To this question I answered an emphatic "yes." Both Scripture and personal experience have convinced me that this is the case. It is generally understood that Satan led a third of the angels in rebellion against God prior to the fall of man (Rev. 12:4). Scripture speaks of an innumerable host of holy angels that did not rebel against God (Rev. 5:11). Thus, the number of fallen angels (demons, unclean spirits, foul spirits, spirits of divination, etc.) is enormous. In conclusion, there are plenty of evil spirits to wreak havoc upon our lives. This matter of spiritual warfare cannot be downplayed; it is serious, and it is real.

The author has been subjected to mental and momentary physical oppression by satanic forces. While visiting remote areas of China, I have witnessed poor souls either indwelt or violently oppressed by demonic forces. I recall one young woman, who had been in a Bible study the entire morning, suddenly become harassed (perhaps indwelt) by an evil spirit(s) shortly after lunch. Her countenance became blank and distorted. She suddenly began to hyperventilate, chant gibberish, and sway back in forth in her seat. She was completely incoherent. We carried her to a bed where she thrashed about while Christian hymns were sung and prayers were uttered on her behalf for several hours. At the end of this time, she regained complete composure. The next day, I watched the same episode occur again at exactly the same time of day. The procedure of the preceding day was again repeated. This affliction occurred daily for over two weeks until many Christians gathered about this woman for a non-stop 18-hour season of prayer. She soon trusted Christ as her Lord and Savior and has not experienced the before mentioned suffering since.

The Apostle Paul describes how God, through our spirit, clashes with both satanic opposition and with our own flesh in the mind battlefield.

> *For though we walk in the flesh, we do not war after the flesh: (for the weapons of our warfare are not carnal, but mighty through God to the pulling down of strong holds;)* ***casting down imaginations****, and every high thing that exalteth itself against the knowledge of God, and bringing into captivity* ***every thought*** *to the obedience of Christ* (2 Cor. 10:3-5).

> *In whom the god of this world [Satan]* ***hath blinded the minds of them which believe not,*** *lest the light of the glorious gospel of Christ, who is the image of God, should shine unto them* (2 Cor. 4:4).

Paul describes to us the battle, where it is being fought, and the objectives of the enemy – to control the mind and to win over the whole person to his cause. Satan does not initially have control over the body, the heart or the will, but as the mind allows him to invade and to intrude, strongholds and bents are established. All solicitations to sin by Satan are presented to the mind though the flesh, the heart or the will may help secure the consent of the mind. Satan carefully aims temptation at the mind in the form of thoughts. Thoughts and temptations cannot be separated from one another; the former represents the medium, the latter the intent. In the case of Satan, the intent is always evil, thus the thought will have this purpose. The murderous gun may have fired the bullet to inflict death, but it was evil intent that pulled the trigger. If the mind deflects these incoming thoughts, no ill is accomplished in his or her person.

In a sense, the mind succumbs to the flesh, and allows the enemy to "dig in" and to establish fortifications within our being. The enemy erects invisible bastions of lust and bunkers of self-wantonness within our body and soul. From these strongholds, incoming suggestions and temptations are empowered and strengthened. This coordinated alliance batters man's spirit without mercy. When firmly held in Satan's grasp, the human mind becomes hardened and reprobate. An individual in this state will follow the natural desires of his flesh and his depraved mind – the voice of the human spirit is ignored. The believer has the aid of the Holy Spirit to pull down proud arguments and to rule over the lusting cries of the flesh. The unregenerate, however, have only one resource to combat the wiles of the devil – the still quiet voice of their spirit that continually pleads God's truth to the mind.

When Satan establishes a stronghold in the mind, the only solution is spiritual and mental warfare that will aggressively attack every rebellious thought and captivate it to the obedience of Christ. This is serious business – Satan is battling for your mind. We will not be able to outsmart him or utilize human ingenuity to overcome citadels in our thinking. Strongholds are negative patterns of thought that get entrenched into our minds through repetition or trauma (e.g. emotional, verbal, physical, or sexual abuse). Repetitive wrong thinking or wrong behavior digs a trench, one shovel full at a time, while trauma better resembles blasting with dynamite and then falling into the consequential hole. As the thoughts are captivated one by one, a stronghold is diminished and is eventually pulled down and destroyed. The enemy's garrison loses strength and finally has no more power to oppress the believer and thus collapses.

Factors in Spiritual Warfare

No matter what type of enemy you are confronting, there are basic principles that apply universally to military strategy: intelligence information must identify the enemy, his location and capabilities, and determine the best battle plan for victory. These strategies apply to spiritual welfare as well. The Bible is our intelligence report. The Author of the Bible created and intimately knows the enemy, so the information is valid. The Bible solicits all soldiers of the cross to:

1. Know the enemy (1 Pet. 5:8; Eph. 6:12)
2. Know the enemy's devices (2 Cor. 2:11)
3. Be mature in using spiritual weapons (Eph. 6:11; 1 Thess. 5:8)
4. Know the application of spiritual weapons (Eph. 6:13-18)

Who is the enemy? Paul and Peter are in complete agreement about this matter.

> *For we wrestle not against flesh and blood, but against principalities, against powers, against the rulers of the darkness of this world, against spiritual wickedness in high places* (Eph. 6:12).

> *Be sober, be vigilant; because your adversary the devil, as a roaring lion, walketh about, seeking whom he may devour* (1 Pet. 5:8).

The enemy of our souls is not the atheist next door, or the Muslim in the Middle East. Satan is the adversary of God (Matt. 4:10, 12:26; Mk. 1:13, 3:23, 26), of God's people (Lk. 22:31; Acts 5:3; Rom. 16:20; 1 Cor. 5:5, 7:5; 2 Cor. 2:11,

11:14, 12:7), and of mankind (Lk. 13:16; Acts 26:18; 2 Thess. 2:9; Rev. 12:9, 20:7). Our sole enemy is Satan and his evil cohorts in crime.

Satan, before his rebellion, was formally called Lucifer, meaning "light bearer." Lucifer was created in perfection (Ezek. 28:12-15). He was an anointed (specially chosen) cherub. As a cherub, he was created with four faces and four wings (Ezek. 1). According to Ezekiel 28:13, Lucifer was created with every precious stone as a covering and had a provision of timbrels and flutes to make music before God. In the celestial realms, music accompanied the worship of spiritual beings before the throne of God, even before man was created. But Satan's inflated pride motivated in him a desire to be worshipped, and, consequently, God thrust him off His holy mount (Isa. 14:12-17). Thus, the "light bearer" became the "father of darkness." Satan and the demons know their final destiny – the lake of fire (Matt. 25:41; Rev. 12:12; Lk. 4:34, 8:28). Their doom, sealed by Christ at Calvary, is foretold in stages (Lk. 10:18; Rev. 20:2, 10).

What type of character does Satan exhibit? He always lies (Jn. 8:44); he is deceitful (2 Cor. 11:13); he is proud (Isa. 14:11-14), and he becomes easily angered (Rev. 12:12). He cannot create life (Ex. 8:16-19; Jn. 1:3-4), but thoroughly enjoys ending physical life (Matt. 24:22; Rev. 13:7, 15). He encourages humans to rebel against God and to follow him into eternal death (Gen. 3; Rev. 13). Because Satan desires to be like God he often resorts to mimicking God and His work. Christ has a bride (the church – Eph. 5; Rev. 19:7-8), and during the tribulation period, Satan will have his woman too – a harlot (Rev. 17). After the rapture of the church, Satan gets all the unbelievers left behind to form "the mother of harlots and abominations on earth" (Rev. 17:5). His woman is the one-world religion that will be the culmination of all pagan, anti-

God religions of the world under one umbrella. God is triune, so Satan has his unholy trinity: himself, the Anti-Christ and the False Prophet (Rev. 13). The Anti-Christ may counterfeit a resurrection during the tribulation period according to Revelation 13:5. Satan is a deceiver, a slanderer, a liar, a mimic of God, and in general, the archenemy of our souls.

> *For such are false apostles, <u>deceitful</u> workers, transforming themselves into the apostles of Christ. And no marvel; **for Satan himself is transformed into an angel of light**. Therefore it is no great thing if his ministers also be transformed as the ministers of righteousness; whose end shall be according to their works* (2 Cor. 11:13-15).

> *Ye are of your father the devil, and the lusts of your father ye will do. He was a murderer from the beginning, and abode not in the truth, because **there is no truth in him**. When he speaketh a lie, he speaketh of his own: for he is a liar, and the father of it* (Jn. 8:44).

The Apostle Paul warns believers concerning Satan's activity: "Lest Satan should get an advantage of us: for we are not ignorant of his devices" (2 Cor. 2:11). What evil devices does Satan inflict upon humanity? He organizes dire circumstances within our lives to test us (Jam. 1:13). However, these trials are within the realm of divine boundaries (1 Cor. 10:13; Job 1) and are for the purpose of building our faith. Satan is the "god of this age" (2 Cor. 4:4), the prince of this world (Jn. 12:31, 14:30, 16:11), and "the prince of the power of the air" (Eph. 2:2). For a time, God has directly delegated authority to him, for the purpose of influencing the world after his own intentions. In 2 Corinthians, Paul warns of Satan's operations to **blind** the unsaved from seeing the truth (4:4), to **beguile** (divert) believers from sound doctrine (11:3), and to physically **buffet** those holding fast to the faith (12:7).

Satan wants to maximize his evil playground by preserving as much of the corrupted and cursed creation as possible, including our fallen nature. As the believer presently dwells in the world, Satan's temptations initially focus on the body, which is "world-conscious." His desire is to obtain a beachhead of fleshly indulgence as a means to gain further penetration into our souls. From these strongholds, war against the spirit is waged on the battlefield of the mind. If Satan can overpower the mind from these fortifications, the spirit will be denied of a governing influence.

If the devil cannot entangle the believer in direct sin, he will resort to a defensive posture to ensure the believer is no threat to his eroding empire. He accomplishes this by convincing Christians to hold onto as much of the old nature and condemned world as possible, thus preventing yieldedness, which in turn restricts spiritual fruit bearing. Although the believer is not usually enticed to sin outright, Satan effectively confuses and deceives the Christian into loving his old life. The "self life," and not the "spirit life," is ruling.

In addition to inflicting humans with adverse circumstances and a corrupt world system, the author would suggest three main avenues of direct and personal satanic assault: possession, oppression, and obsession. Praise be to God! Christ came to deliver those oppressed by Satan (Acts 10:38).

Possession

Possession occurs when an unbeliever is indwelt by a demon, or demons. These demons gain direct control of the body and the mind, much the same way commandos would forcibly gain control over a weakened military installation. Several missionaries have reported a common observation in possession cases – glaring eyes.[1] Normally individuals are cognizant of their surroundings and have alert eyes, whereas those suffering madness commonly stare blankly into space with dull eyes. However, a possessed individual often projects a penetrating glare, powerfully reflecting the intense hatred and rage within. The believer may witness demon possession, but he cannot be possessed himself. If the Holy Spirit has sealed (Eph. 1:13) and taken up residence in an individual (1 Cor. 6:19), He will in no way relinquish that vessel for Satan's inhabitation. Therefore, a believer cannot be indwelt by demons, but the oppression that demons can inflict upon a vulnerable or carnal believer may indeed lead to behavior that seems to an observer much like that of a possessed individual.

Oppression

Oppression can speak of a wide range of internal and external influences that Satan may bring to bear on humanity. In respect to the believer, these are external influences that try the patience of our faith. Job is a classic example in the Bible of obvious physical and mental oppression.

Satan not only inflicted Paul's body, but also hindered him from visiting the Christians at Thessalonica.

> *And lest I should be exalted above measure through the abundance of the revelations, there was given to me a thorn in the flesh, the messenger of **Satan to buffet me**, lest I should be exalted above measure (2 Cor. 12:7).*

> *Wherefore we would have come unto you, even I Paul, once and again; **but Satan hindered us** (1 Thess. 2:18).*

Watchman Nee notes:
The emotional part of the soul also can be aroused easily by the adversary. Since many believers crave joyful feel-

ings and the sensations of having the Holy Spirit, of the loveliness of the Lord Jesus, and of the presence of God, evil spirits will supply their senses with many strange experiences. This is that their natural abilities might be stimulated and that the still small voice of the Holy Spirit, traceable only by man's delicate intuitive faculty in his spirit, might be suppressed.[2]

Obsession

Obsession is the direct injection of evil thoughts into the human mind. Paul acknowledges that there is *a "spirit that is now at work in the sons of disobedience"* (Eph. 2:2). This is not possession or external oppression. Obsession is a tool used by Satan to mentally torment believers. The enemy may plant thoughts to lure us into establishing a stronghold in the flesh (such as pornography), or he may observe a self-erected stronghold in the heart, such as bitterness, and seek to stir up unforgiving thoughts. Satan or his cohorts in crime then stimulate these strongholds with ungodly thoughts to inflict anxiety, distress, and depression. If there were no strongholds (i.e. bitterness, anger, envy, etc.), Satan's efforts of obsessing the believer's mind would be ineffective, and he would soon terminate the mental attack (Jas. 4:7).

I liken obsessing the believer's mind to a spinning merry-go-round, where the circular energy represents a built-up stronghold (the energy of a bent not confessed and repented of). Though Satan does not have the energy to start the merry-go-round spinning, he can keep it (the stronghold) whirling by suggestions much like a child on the playground continues to grab and pull the bars of the merry-go-round to maintain rotation. However, when the believer resists by renewing his or her mind (or figuratively drags his or her feet in the illustration), the merry-go-round slowly stops until Satan realizes his efforts are futile and departs. The stronghold has lost its hold. Matthew Henry comments on this subject (referring to Jas. 4:7):

> We are taught to submit ourselves entirely to God: "Submit yourselves therefore to God. Resist the devil, and he will flee from you" (verse 7). Christians should forsake the friendship of the world, and watch against that envy and pride which they see prevailing in natural men, and should by grace learn to glory in their submission to God. ... Now, as this subjection and submission to God are what the devil most industriously strives to hinder, so we ought with great care and steadiness to resist his suggestions. If he would represent a tame yielding to the will and providence of God as what will bring calamities, and expose to contempt and misery, we must **resist these suggestions** of fear. If he would represent submission to God as a hindrance to our outward ease, or worldly preferments, we must **resist these suggestions** of pride and sloth. If he would tempt us to lay any of our miseries, and crosses, and afflictions, to the charge of Providence, so that we might avoid them by following his directions instead of God's, we must resist these provocations to anger, not fretting ourselves in any wise to do evil. "Let not the devil, in these or the like attempts, prevail upon you; but resist him and he will flee from you." If we basely yield to temptations, the devil will continually follow us; but if we put on the whole armor of God, and stand it out against him, he will be gone from us. Resolution shuts and bolts the door against temptation.[3]

Ananias is the excellent example of satanic obsession targeting the mind. Apparently, a stronghold existed in the heart of this believer (Acts 5).

> *But Peter said, "Ananias, why **hath Satan filled thine heart to lie to the Holy Ghost**, and to keep back part of the price of the land?"* (Acts 5:3).

Again Matthew Henry comments: "The origin of his sin: Satan filled his heart; he not only suggested it to him, and put it into his head, but hurried him on with resolution to do it."[4]

Stanley D. Toussaint provides the following insight on the same passage of Scripture.

> In response Peter accused Ananias by saying, Satan has … filled your heart. The verb translated "filled" is *eplerosen*, from *pleroo*, which here has the idea of control or influence. The same verb is used in the command, "Be filled with the Spirit" (Eph. 5:18). Ananias, a believer, was influenced by Satan, not the Spirit! The fact that Peter asked, "How is it …?" implies that Satan had gained control because Ananias had not dealt with some previous sin in his life.[5]

Warren Wiersbe also comments on Acts 5:

> To begin with, the sin of Ananias and Sapphira was energized by Satan; and that is a serious matter. If Satan cannot defeat the church by attacks from the outside, he will get on the inside and go to work (Acts 20:28-31). He knows how to lie to the minds and the hearts of church members, even genuine Christians, and get them to follow his orders.[6]

Because Ananias had not previously repented and gained the victory over "soulish bents" (perhaps pride or envy), Satan was able to stimulate these strongholds through obsession. He injected musings into Ananias' mind that energized these controlling bents. If Ananias had renewed his mind and drawn near to God through obedience, there would not have been any strongholds for Satan to victimize. Consequently, the adversary would have fled from Ananias and scurried off to trouble someone else (Jas. 4:7).

It must be emphasized that Satan is not the direct source of all tempting thoughts. He may externally assault our minds with evil thoughts, or indirectly use an evil world system that opposes God. *"For all that is in the world, the lust of the flesh [body appetites], and the lust of the eyes [coveting], and the pride of life [self glory], is not of the Father, but is of the world"* (1 Jn. 2:16). The surrounding world system under his control stimulates our members to respond contrary to our spirit's order. Lustfulness, selfishness and vain ambition do not proceed from the Father, but from the world. As a result of these secular influences, our own flesh bombards the mind with appeals for satisfaction. Our heart and soul lust and envy for self-exalting acknowledgement. The majority of the time sin occurs because the mind surrenders to the pull of our members instead of the petitions of our spirit as pled by the Holy Spirit.

For the good that I would I do not: but the evil which I would not, that I do. Now if I do that I would not, it is no more I that do it, but sin that dwelleth in me. I find then a law, that, when I would do good, evil is present with me. For I delight in the law of God after the inward man: But I see another law in my members, warring against the law of my mind, and bringing me into captivity to the law of sin which is in my members. O wretched man that I am! Who shall deliver me from the body of this death? I thank God through Jesus Christ our Lord. So then with the mind I myself serve the law of God; but with the flesh the law of sin (Rom. 7:19-25).

Satan probably appreciates us accrediting him with all our failures and sinfulness. The activity bestows upon him vain-glory in confronting the purposes of God. The believer's purpose in life, however, is to bestow glory upon God through righteousness, not the enemy through sin. Blame-shifting only denies personal responsibility for our offenses and hinders spiritual growth. Restoration with God requires repentance (1 Jn. 1:9). True repentance acknowledges what was offensive to God, accepts personal responsibility for the damage, grieves over the crime, then turns from the ill behavior. So how can one determine if unrighteous thoughts are being generated from within our members or externally through satanic obsession? Watchman Nee explains:

> The believer may shake his head repeatedly, yet he cannot shake off the thoughts in his mind. They come to him in waves, rolling unceasingly day and night. There is no way to terminate them. He is not aware that this is but the activity of the evil spirit. He ought to understand what a "thought" is. It is something which his *mind grasps at*. But in the case of these unmanageable thoughts it is not that his mind is grasping at something but rather that *something is grasping his mind*. In the natural course of events it is the mind which thinks about matters; now it is these matters which force the mind to think. Frequently a person wishes to set aside a matter but some external power keeps reminding him of it, nor permitting him to forget and forcing him to think on further. This is the perpetration of evil spirits.[7]

Satanic obsession is not easily shaken off; whereas, internally generated desires are more easily transformed and brought into submission to Jesus Christ. Through renewing the mind, strongholds are pulled down, and what was haunting the

mind and warring against the spirit is illuminated. With obsession, mental taunting seems endless. You can't escape the
thought no matter what you do. Before long your sleep is affected, your stomach acids are always churned up, and you live
in a state of exhaustion and mental fatigue. Forgetfulness, inat-
tentiveness, inactivity, and isolation will characterize your life.

The resolution to obsession is found in completely casting
one's self before the throne of grace and persistently pleading
the blessed Savior for assistance. Only through the power of
the Holy Spirit can one stand in faith and resist the temptation.
*"God resisteth the proud, but giveth grace unto the humble.
Submit yourselves, therefore, to God. Resist the devil, and he
will flee from you. Draw near to God, and He will draw near to
you..."* (Jam. 4:6-8).

> He is able to deliver thee, though by sin oppressed,
> Go to Him for rest, our God is able to deliver thee.

> William A. Ogden

Obsession becomes more obvious when the assault is over.
The mental release that follows obsession is warmly welcomed. Because the believer has co-labored with the Lord to
resist and to defeat the attacker, the freshness of the Lord's
presence is especially sweet. The threatening clouds of darkness that loomed overhead for so long suddenly disperse, and
the welcomed glorious sunshine of Almighty God fills our
hearts anew. As you ponder the past incident, you wonder why
you even had those thoughts or why the situation had such a
hold on you – it just doesn't make sense. The reason is that the
thoughts were not generated from within.

The author cannot highlight enough the importance of holy
living, renewing the mind, and the power of prayer to combat

the offensive engagements of the enemy. If you're living "carnally," you will be easy prey. If you do not renew your mind continually, expect mental harassment to be rendered effectively by the enemy. If you do not boldly approach the throne of grace through prayer, you will have no strength to combat the enemy.

A dear brother in China accentuated this point after we had both been physically harassed by demons for a brief period outside a Buddhist temple in China. Shortly after being released, he turned to me and said, "Now you know why I must pray much every morning – prayer is our only strength here against evil spirits."

A final word concerning visions. Many people are seeing visions and hearing voices these days. Certainly, Satan mimics God's means of declaring revelation (2 Cor. 11:14). In the Old Testament and during the Apostolic Age, prophecy, visions, dreams, and audible commands were prevalent to express divine revelation. Yet, today we must realize that God is speaking in His Son (Heb. 1:2). The Lord Jesus Christ is the Father's ultimate revelation to the world (Jn. 1:1-2, 1:14). Christ has not left us in the dark concerning truth; He has declared to us the divine revelation needed for salvation, godly living, and bringing Him glory. This revelation was brought by the Apostles for us to follow (Heb. 2:3) and is complete in declaration (Jude 3).

With this said, God is God, and He can do anything He pleases. It is suggested that if the reader does witness some supernatural manifestation, the following checklist should be reviewed to determine the source of the event.

1. All that flows from God will agree with His nature and His previously declared Word – Scripture.

2. Based on the pattern of New Testament Scripture, revelation was conferred only to individuals who had consecrated themselves to holy living (e.g. Joseph, Mary, Simeon, Anna, Stephen, Paul, etc.).

3. Visions from the Holy Spirit will occur when the believer's mind is fully active and not hindered by medications, drugs, fatigue, etc. The opposite is true with evil spirits; thus, drug abuse is common in witchcraft and satanic rituals. It is noted that the Greek word *pharmakeia* (from which "pharmacy" is derived) is actually translated "witchcraft" or "sorceries" in the Bible (Gal. 5:20; Rev. 9:21).

4. Not only does God choose to convey revelation when our minds are active, but also when it has a strong focus on the spirit voice. There will be no strongholds within which Satan will use to hinder the voice of God.

5. Is the revelation confusing or coercing you into some immediate action? God does not interject revelation upon us in such a way that we are reduced to mindless puppets. His communication is through our spirit and is patient, clear, exact, and righteous. Paul prayed for the Ephesian Christians "that the Father of glory may give unto you the spirit of wisdom, and revelation in the knowledge of him, the eyes of your understanding being enlightened that ye may know what is the hope of his calling..." (Eph. 1:17-18). God is patient and wants us to understand and be confirmed in our mind as to what is right before action is taken (Rom. 14:23). Satan is the high-pressure salesman!

So if you do witness such an event, ask yourself these questions: Does what I saw or heard agree with God's character and His Word? Am I living purely before God with all strongholds removed from within? Is my mind fully active and in tune with my spirit which intently listens to the Holy Spirit? Is the vision unclear, unholy, and demanding immediate action without allowing me to consider it? God does not want our faith to be based on sensory perception (Heb. 11:3; Jn. 20:29), for Satan can easily manipulate this realm. The author believes this type of divine manifestations will be quite rare to believers.

We have identified the enemy, his evil character, his sinister tactics and his destructive objectives. In the next chapter we will visit the subject of using spiritual armor and weapons to confront the enemy.

Spiritual Mind Frames

Have you heard someone say, "I'm in no frame of mind to handle this problem right now" or "I'm in the wrong frame of mind to talk about this presently?" Our minds are often not prepared for those irritating or contrary situations that so often impose themselves upon us. Delivering the right spiritual response to a particular situation depends on having the proper frame of mind. Paul informed the Christians at Thessalonica that *"... the very **God of peace sanctify you wholly;** and I pray God your whole spirit and soul and body be preserved blameless unto the coming of our Lord Jesus Christ"* (1 Thess. 5:23). It is God's desire that we, in our entirety, be "set apart" for His purpose, including our minds. As the believer's mind is one of the primary focuses of satanic assault, it stands to reason that the mind should be strengthened defensively and ready to minister a spiritually offensive response where possible.

In previous chapters, we looked at mental exercises to strengthen the mind's ability to have the proper spiritual focus when difficulties arise and at the methods by which Satan may infect the mind. The goal of the previous mental exercises is to obtain a fortified mind, where the spirit rules and commands the entire body when aggression approaches either from within or without.

In this chapter, we will utilize a particular mind frame to invoke a spiritual response from the Holy Spirit through the window of the soul. In this way, God reaches His hand out with heaven's glories into the physical realm to address and to resolve threatening situations. Wrong thinking and behavior quenches or grieves the Holy Spirit within the believer (Eph. 4:30; 1 Thess. 5:19). Submission and holy behavior enable Spirit filling (Eph. 5:17-18) which enable the believer to pour out the blessings of God to others. Proper mind frames enable the believer to think as Christ would in various situations. This ensures that the Holy Spirit will not be hindered from operations, thus allowing the infusing power of God to pass through the believer as electricity passes through wire.

Some mind frames are less effective than others in spiritual warfare, given a particular situation. For example, "rejoicing" in difficult circumstances is more effective than "love." Or if the attack is deception, prayer alone is not the best offensive response. The believer must learn to choose a proper mind frame in spiritual combat to be victorious. Selecting a cruise missile for hand-to-hand combat is inappropriate. Wielding a knife to defend an incoming mortar shell will prove to be fatal. Often believers fail in spiritual warfare due to an incorrect response to the attack. The two questions before us are: "How would Jesus Christ respond to such situations?" and "Would I respond like Jesus?"

Proper Mind Frames for Spiritual Warfare

Finally, my brethren, be strong in the Lord, and in the power of his might. Put on the whole armour of God, that ye may be able to stand against the wiles of the devil. For we wrestle not against flesh and blood, but against principalities, against powers, against the rulers of the darkness of this world, against spiritual wickedness in

high places. Wherefore take unto you the whole armour
of God, that ye may be able to withstand in the evil day,
and having done all, to stand. Stand therefore, having
your loins girded about with truth, and having on the
breastplate of righteousness; And your feet shod with the
preparation of the gospel of peace; above all, taking the
shield of faith, wherewith ye shall be able to quench all
the fiery darts of the wicked. And take the helmet of sal-
vation, and the sword of the Spirit, which is the Word of
God: Praying always with all prayer and supplication in
the Spirit, and watching thereunto with all perseverance
and supplication for all saints; and for me, that utterance
may be given unto me, that I may open my mouth boldly,
to make known the mystery of the gospel, for which I am
an ambassador in bonds: that therein I may speak boldly,
as I ought to speak (Eph. 6:10-20).

The following list of spiritual armor is derived from the
above Scripture: loins girded with truth, breastplate of righteousness, feet shod with the preparation of the gospel, shield of
faith, helmet of salvation, sword of the Spirit (which is the
Word of God) – and then the warrior's resource of prayer is
identified. The author would suggest that Paul is providing an
introduction into spiritual warfare and the appropriate spiritual
armor for defense. Ephesians 6 is Spiritual Warfare 101. The
passage contains vital information for the soldier of the cross,
but does not contain all of what Scripture teaches on the subject. It is not an exhaustive list of the spiritual weapons available to the believer.

Ephesians 6 would perhaps be the first place a young believer would go to learn about the enemy of his soul and what
he must do to defend himself against attack. It is an easy passage of Scripture to find. But as a believer matures in Christ,
endures trials, and continues probing God's Word ever more

deeply, he or she becomes aware of other kinds of spiritual weaponry at his or her disposal. These are not as obvious as the list in Ephesians 6 – only the maturing believer will appreciate and benefit. For example, does a wise parent tell their two-year-old, "Help yourself to a paring knife to peel and cut up your apple?" No, the toddler is not capable of performing such a task without hurting himself. Likewise, the army doesn't put a new recruit in a tank and say "go to war." Using spiritual armor and weapons properly requires maturity and training.

Using Mind Frames as Spiritual Weapons

Paul identifies at least ten "mind frames" in his closing remarks to the church at Thessalonica. These Christians were young in the Lord, but already battle-hardened soldiers of the cross. In just the short interval since Paul had departed from them, they had experienced persecution, but were persevering by God's grace (1 Thess. 1:6). Paul highlights to these believers a check-list of basic equipment to utilize while in the fray of spiritual battle. Just as a soldier in the infantry has a checklist of basic equipment and survival gear, Paul reminds them of basic mental frames to invoke spiritual power in battle. The proper use of these mind persuasions allows the Holy Spirit unhindered opportunity to secure victory and to present our whole being blameless and sanctified for God's use. The mind has no strength of its own to enlist spiritual power, but it can hinder the Holy Spirit from working effectively.

> *But let us, who are of the day, be sober, putting on the breastplate of faith and love; and for an helmet, the hope of salvation* (1 Thess. 5:8).

Rejoice evermore. Pray without ceasing. In everything give thanks: for this is the will of God in Christ Jesus concerning you. Quench not the Spirit. Despise not prophesyings. Prove all things; hold fast that which is good. Abstain from all appearance of evil. And the very God of peace sanctify you wholly; and I pray God your whole spirit and soul and body be preserved blameless unto the coming of our Lord Jesus Christ (1 Thess. 5:16-23).

The Love Frame (v. 8)

As we have therefore opportunity, let us do good unto all men, especially unto them who are of the household of faith (Gal. 6:10).

But I say unto you, love your enemies, bless them that curse you, do good to them that hate you, and pray for them which despitefully use you, and persecute you (Matt. 5:44).

Recompense to no man evil for evil. Provide things honest in the sight of all men. If it be possible, as much as lieth in you, live peaceably with all men. Dearly beloved, avenge not yourselves, but rather give place unto wrath: for it is written, Vengeance is mine; I will repay, saith the Lord. Therefore if thine enemy hunger, feed him; if he thirst, give him drink: for in so doing thou shalt heap coals of fire on his head. Be not overcome of evil, but overcome evil with good (Rom. 12:17-21).

Paul instructed the Christians in Rome to *"Owe no man any thing, but to love one another: for he that loveth another hath fulfilled the law"* (Rom. 13:8). Earlier in his epistle to them he declared that the purpose of the law was to show that man was sinful and needed a Savior – Christ (Rom. 3:20-25). If someone stole something, it proved that they could not "keep" the law and were sinful. The law declares God's holiness and man's depraved state. But once the Holy Spirit indwells a believer, he or she becomes able to "fulfill" the law. When one chooses not to steal, that is keeping the law; but fulfilling the law is not just "don't steal" from another, it is giving to that person. Giving expresses love. God's holiness is reflected in keeping the law, but His gracious character is represented in fulfilling the law. Through the power of the Holy Spirit, the believer conveys the love of God to others in a supernatural way. It is not natural to love our enemies, to do good to those who persecute us, to bless those who curse us, or to withhold vengeance when it is just.

The believer should never be satisfied with his outward projection of God's love. Can a husband love his wife too much? No, he will never love his wife as Christ loves the church (Eph. 5:25). Thus there will always be room to abound more and more. The church at Thessalonica was thriving in the midst of Jewish persecution, yet Paul exhorts, *"And the Lord make you to increase and abound in love one toward another, and toward all men, even as we do toward you"*(1 Thess. 3:12). The Lord would receive the most glory; they would receive the most joy, and the Holy Spirit would accomplish the most blessing when they chose to invoke a mind frame of love to address "people problems." In this way, love is a spiritual weapon.

How does one "put on" love (1 Thess. 5:8)? Paul gives further instruction in the use of the love mind frame, "See that none render evil for evil unto any man; but ever follow that which is good, both among yourselves, and to all men" (1 Thess. 5:15). Yes, rejoice in the Lord and pray, but when "people troubles" are overwhelming you, resort to love. The more you are hated – the more you should love. Usually, in God's time, the oppressor will break down – because God's love is irresistible.

We once had an unsaved neighbor whose demeanor towards our family was unjustly harsh. We bore this plight, as did many of our surrounding neighbors. We directed a consistent stream of kindness to our rude and caustic neighbor for seven years without a favorable response. However, on one frigid morning after a significant snowfall, our grumpy neighbor surprised us by arriving at our home with his tractor. Without saying a word he promptly cleared away the snow from our long driveway. Our family watched from the living room picture window in disbelief. I turned to the children and said, "See guys, love really does work." When he was finished, I ventured outdoors to thank him and to hand him a cup of coffee. I will never forget his words – "I just wanted to say thank you for being nice neighbors." God's love in action is a wonderful resource to bring even the vilest sinner to his knees.

If you have love, you are not only going to think no evil, you're going to take your tongue and have it nailed to the cross so that you bless instead of curse.

Billy Graham

Love is the only service that power cannot command and money cannot buy.

Susan Polis Schutz

As a Spiritual Weapon: If your difficulties relate to people problems, always use the mind frame of love. Through this mind frame, the irresistible love of God will flow and melt even the most hardened and crusty hearts!

The Faith Frame (v. 8)

Faith defeats doubt. Faith is likened to both a breastplate (1 Thess. 5:8) and a shield (Eph. 6:16). Both are defensive pieces of armor, which if effectively used, prevent pointed objects from penetrating into the inner man. A strong faith deflects suggestive thoughts that would overwhelm the soul with doubt. This mind frame peers backward to review God's past faithfulness and then surges forward in trust. God upholds the "big picture" no matter how grueling the outward appearance might seem. By gazing backward to God's faithfulness, one is able to progress forward in faith.

This mind frame helped Abraham defeat any doubts that buffeted his mind concerning the commanded sacrifice of Isaac (Gen. 22). God had shown Himself faithful in the past; therefore, Abraham had a firm foundation to again grasp God's promise by faith. God had promised to create a special nation of people through his son Isaac. How firm of faith did Abraham have? Hebrews 11:19 explains:

> *By faith Abraham, when he was tried, offered up Isaac: and he that had received the promises offered up his only begotten son, of whom it was said, that in Isaac shall thy seed be called: Accounting that God was able to raise him up, even from the dead; from whence also he received him in a figure* (Heb. 11:17-19).

Abraham knew that if he struck Isaac down, God would raise him back up again, for he was the son of promise. Since there had never been a resurrection from the dead before, how could Abraham trust God so fully? Because Abraham knew his God and His past faithfulness. The Lord had safeguarded Abraham and his family while journeying a thousand miles through unknown terrain and dangers. The Lord had delivered him from overwhelming military odds: Pharaoh and the empire of Egypt (Gen. 12), attacking Eastern armies (Gen. 14), and Abimelech and the Philistines (Gen. 20). God told Abraham in Genesis 12 that He would greatly bless him and to "Fear not, Abram: I am thy shield, and thy exceedingly great reward" (Gen. 15:1). God's past faithfulness allowed Abram to press forward in confidence.

> Faith for my deliverance is not faith in God. Faith means, whether I am visibly delivered or not, I will stick to my belief that God is love. There are some things only learned in a fiery furnace.
>
> Faith is deliberate confidence in the character of God whose ways you cannot understand at the time.
>
> Oswald Chambers

God's faithfulness is beautifully symbolized by a circular rainbow about His heavenly throne. A rainbow was bestowed to mankind as a testimony to God's promise never to flood the entire earth again (Gen. 9:13), while a circle pictures eternity and endless reality. God demonstrates, through these compound symbols, that His promises are kept for eternity; He never rescinds or voids His promises to us. Remember, He promised never to leave, or to forsake us (Heb. 13:5), or to allow more testing than we can bear without providing grace or a way of escape (1 Cor. 10:13). Paul reminded the suffering young Thessalonian Christians, *"Faithful is He that calleth you, who also will do it"* (1 Thess. 5:24). And he reminded Timothy, *"If we believe not, yet He abideth faithful: He cannot deny Himself"* (2 Tim. 2:13). A true living trust in God of this type repels doubt.

Paul also encouraged the Thessalonians to "comfort the feebleminded, support the weak" (1 Thess. 5:14). Often the faith of others is needed to strengthen the fainthearted (Heb. 11). The "shield of faith" (Eph. 6:16) was related to the Roman leather-covered wooden shield (about four feet high and two feet wide) which could be connected with the shield of the other soldiers to create an impenetrable wall against incoming fiery darts and arrows. There is strength in numbers, and the faith of the many can "pull up" those wobbly-kneed believers that are under crushing loads (Gal. 6:2). Christians need each other, and we need each other's faith to carry on boldly for the Lord. We all suffer at times with mental weakness. Doubts pour over us like a flood. But praise God for those who will come alongside and lift our heads heavenward. Paul was contained behind prison bars, but his faith could not be constrained. As a result, others were "much more bold to speak the word without fear" (Phil. 1:14). May our faith have a Christ focus and be a benefit to His body – the church.

Although Charles Haddon Spurgeon was well known as the "Prince of Preachers," very little is known of his wife, who suffered many physical trials for nearly thirty years of her life. Once she wrote:

> At the close of a dark and gloomy day, I lay resting on my couch as the deeper night drew on ... and some of the darkness seemed to have entered into my soul.

Vainly I tried to see the hand which I knew held mine, and guided my fog-enveloped feet along a steep and slippery path of suffering. 'Why does my Lord ... so often send sharp and bitter pain? Why does He permit lingering weakness to hinder the sweet service I long to render?' For a while silence reigned, broken only by the crackling of the oak log burning in the fireplace. Suddenly I heard a sweet, soft musical note, like a robin beneath my window. Yet there was no robin. 'It comes from the log on the fire,' my friend exclaimed. The fire was letting loose the imprisoned music from the old oak's inmost heart! The oak had stored up the song in the days when all was well with him, but it took the flames of the fire to consume away the calluses of age to let it out again.[1]

Yes, dear beloved "count it all joy when you fall into various trials, knowing that the testing of your faith produces patience" (Jas. 1:2-3, NKJV). God is faithful and will remain faithful. Faith that is not tested will not be trusted when the trials come, so don't waste a good problem!

> Little faith will take your soul to heaven, but great faith will bring heaven to your soul.
>
> Charles Spurgeon

Not only does exercising faith bring heaven to your soul, it has an effect of ushering others toward heaven. As others witness your triumphal faith in the face of adversity, the believer is encouraged to be more faithful, while the unsaved are prompted to peer into their own void hearts to realize that they are bankrupt of such resources. Justin Martyr, a second century philosopher who converted to Christianity and became a tireless evangelist and apologist, writes:

> It is evident that no one can terrify or subdue us. For, throughout all the word, we have believed in Jesus! It is clear that, although beheaded, and crucified, and thrown to wild beasts ... and fire, and all other kinds of torture, we do not give up our confession. But the more such things happen, the more do other persons and in larger numbers become faithful believers and worshippers of God through the name of Jesus.[2]

The Apostle Paul understood this sacrificial calling; it was the very goal of his faith and demanded nothing less than "always bearing about in the body the dying of the Lord Jesus, that the life also of Jesus might be made manifest in our body. For we who live are always delivered unto death for Jesus' sake, that the life also of Jesus might be made manifest in our mortal flesh" (2 Cor. 4:10-11).

As a Spiritual Weapon: Use faith, as based on God's past faithfulness to His promises, to defeat doubt. Hudson Taylor put it this way, "But how to get faith strengthened? Not by striving after faith, but by resting in the Faithful One."[3] Watchman Nee suggested, "True faith is not about trying, it is about dying and learning to walk in His love. The truth is that the more you try to deal with inner dryness, depression, and flatness, the more you cannot overcome them. These things become an issue because we make them an issue. If you forget about them and let them go, they will disappear."[4] Faith allows God to effectively work a solution in your life that is beyond anything you could imagine. Faith waits for God's deliverance with joy and for a solution that bestows wider blessing to more people.

The Hope Frame (v. 8)

To the Ephesian believers Paul spoke of the necessity of wearing the helmet of salvation (Eph. 6:17), but to the Christians at Thessalonica he further identified what the helmet of salvation is – "the hope of salvation" (1 Thess. 5:8). As the faith mind frame gazes backwards in time to God's prior faithfulness, the hope mind frame peers forward with joyful expectation. Hope clutches to God's promises, reckons them true and personal, and then completely trusts God for their fulfillment. Hope is used to defeat discouragement by providing present comfort and joy in a future promise of God. Time passes quickly and joyfully when we are looking forward to something.

The word "hope" is almost exclusively used to speak of the coming of the Lord in the air for His church – the rapture. For there is one hope (Eph. 4:4), and it is *"looking for that blessed hope, and the glorious appearing of the great God and our Saviour Jesus Christ"* (Titus 2:13). This event is the believer's greatest hope. The expectation of imminently and suddenly being "caught up" into the blissful presence of the Lord Jesus should thrill the soul of every believer. John reminds us not to lose sight of this event for not only will thinking about it provide joy during dark times, but it will also promote holy living. *"Beloved, now are we the sons of God, and it doth not yet appear what we shall be: but we know that, when He shall appear, we shall be like Him; for we shall see Him as He is. And every man that hath this hope in him purifieth himself, even as he is pure"* (1 Jn. 3:2-3). The writers of the New Testament lived each and every day in earnest expectation of their blessed hope, being with the Lord Jesus in glory:

John (90AD)
1 John 2:18: *"It is the last times"*

91

1 John 2:28: *"He shall appear that **we** may have confidence and not be ashamed before Him at His coming."*

Paul (60AD)

1 Thessalonians 4:17: *"Then **we** which are alive and remain shall be caught up together with them in the clouds, to meet the Lord in the air: and so shall we ever be with the Lord."*

Philippians 3:20-21: *"Who shall change **our** vile body, that it may be fashioned like unto His glorious body"*

James (45-50 AD)

James 5:8: *"The coming of the Lord draweth nigh"*

Peter (66AD)

2 Peter 3:10-14: *"That ye be looking for the coming day of the Lord"*

1 Peter 4:7: *"But the end of all things is at hand"* (speaking of Christ's coming).

A special reward, "the crown of righteousness" is bequeathed by Christ to all believers who "love His appearing" (2 Tim. 4:8). Three times in the final chapter of the Bible Christ reminds His church, "Behold I come quickly" (Rev. 22:7, 12, 20). Trusting in God's future promises results in present joy. Although Christ's face was set as a flint towards Jerusalem (Isa. 50:7), He had an intense focus beyond the cross. He had God's promise that He would not be left in the grave, but would be exalted to His right hand of majesty on high:

*Therefore My heart is glad, and My glory rejoiceth: **My flesh also shall rest in hope**. For thou wilt not leave My soul in hell; neither wilt Thou suffer Thine Holy One to see corruption. Thou wilt show Me the path of life: in Thy presence is fulness of joy; at Thy right hand there are pleasures for evermore* (Ps. 16:9-11).

*Looking unto Jesus the author and finisher of our faith; **who for the joy that was set before Him endured the cross**, despising the shame, and is set down at the right hand of the throne of God* (Heb 12:2).

The assurance of God's Word brought Christ hope for the future and an infusion of joy while bearing tremendous pain and suffering. His disciples faced death with the same hope and endured tremendous suffering for the joy set before them. History records that Aegeas crucified Andrew, Peter's brother, for his faith in Christ. Seeing his cross before him, Andrew bravely spoke, "O cross, most welcome and longed for! With a willing mind, joyfully and desirously, I come to thee, being the scholar of Him which did hang on thee: because I have always been thy lover, and have coveted to embrace thee."[5] Why could Andrew approach his cross with joy? He watched the Lord approach His cross in the same manner. During the deepest trials of life, it is possible to have present joy in God's future promises.

Assuming personal ownership of God's promises will infuse joy into any situation. *"For we are saved by hope. But hope that is seen is not hope; for what a man seeth, why doth he yet hope for? But if we hope for that which we see not, then do we with patience wait for it"* (Rom. 8:24-25).

Dr. G. Campbell Morgan tells of an experience in his life that illustrates the power of hope in God's promises.

93

Early in his Christian life, Morgan used to visit several ladies once a week to read the Bible to them. When he came to the end of Matthew's Gospel, Morgan read, "Lo, I am with you always, even unto the end of this age." He added, "Isn't that a wonderful promise?" One of the ladies quickly replied, "Young man, that is not a promise—it is a fact!"[6]

As a Spiritual Weapon: Use hope to defeat discouragement. Laying hold of God's promises consoles the soul and promotes joy despite pain and sorrow.

The Rejoicing Frame (v. 16)

Verse 16, "rejoice evermore," is the shortest verse in the Greek New Testament, but one of the most important. Joy removes the burden. God's family should be a happy family, meaning we all must contribute to the atmosphere of joy. There is no room for a "doom and gloom" attitude. *"Yet, if any man suffer as a Christian, let him not be ashamed, but let him glorify God on this behalf"* (1 Pet. 4:16). As a believer chooses to rejoice in the Lord while in the midst of a dire situation, God often glorifies Himself by working a miraculous solution to end the trial. Here are a few examples:

Pagans at Philippi accused Paul and Silas of wrongdoing. They were not extended the right of a fair trial, but instead were beaten, chained, and put into prison. In the inner prison, the air circulation was poor. The stench of open wounds, feces, and body odor that accompanied the smoke from torches ensured difficult breathing. How did these two servants of the Lord respond to this cruel situation? *"And at midnight Paul and Silas prayed, and sang praises unto God; and the prisoners heard them"* (Acts 16:25). They prayed (the right weapon for gospel expansion), and they rejoiced in their God through singing. How did the Lord respond to their praying and rejoicing? He brought a great earthquake, which released them from their captivity and then provided an opportunity for the jailer and his whole family to hear and believe the gospel of Jesus Christ.

How did the apostles respond after they had been arrested and beaten by the Pharisees for preaching Christ?

> *And to him they agreed: and when they had called the apostles, and beaten them, they commanded that they should not speak in the name of Jesus, and let them go. And they departed from the presence of the council, **rejoicing that they were counted worthy to suffer shame for his name**. And daily in the temple, and in every house, they ceased not to teach and preach Jesus Christ* (Acts 5:40-42).

Despite the Pharisees' solemn warning against preaching Christ, the apostles continued preaching and teaching Jesus Christ, and the Church multiplied. Instead of choosing to be depressed or bitter about their stripes, the disciples determined to rejoice in their Savior. It may be that our rejoicing does not specifically or immediately bring relief or conclusion to our difficulty, but God has promised to work a greater good and glorify Himself through every situation (Rom. 8:28). Rejoicing in the Lord demonstrates a trusting faith in God's sovereign control over every matter of life.

Writing to the Corinthians, Paul relates some of the incredible difficulties he faced in his ministry, but then concludes by declaring, *"As sorrowful, yet always rejoicing"* (2 Cor. 6:10). The Lord had miraculously delivered him from many life-threatening circumstances (2 Cor. 11:23-28). He also informed the Corinthians that he had maintained a glad state though his laboring among them had cost him greatly. Paul had a choice to complain or to rejoice in his laboring which in time brought the Corinthians to maturity. Note: *chairo* may be translated as an act of gladness, or rejoicing, or joy as in the following verses:

> *And I will **very gladly** spend and be spent for you; though the more abundantly I love you, the less I be loved* (2 Cor. 12:15).

> *For **we are glad**, when we are weak, and ye are strong: and this also we wish, even your perfection* (2 Cor. 13:9).

The Lord Jesus encourages His disciples to use the spiritual weapon of rejoicing when afflicted with dire circumstances:

> *Blessed are ye, when men shall **hate you**, and when they shall separate you from their company, and shall **reproach you**, and **cast out your name as evil**, for the Son of man's sake. **Rejoice ye in that day, and leap for joy:** for, behold, your reward is great in heaven: for in the like manner did their fathers unto the prophets* (Lk. 6:22-23).

Shortly after building a wall around the entire city of Jerusalem in fifty-two days, Nehemiah declared, "*...neither be ye sorry; **for the joy of the LORD is your strength**"* (Neh. 8:10). The Psalmist writes: *"Delight thyself also in the LORD; and He shall give thee the desires of thine heart"* (Ps. 37:4).

As a Spiritual Weapon: Use "rejoicing" to glorify God through difficult circumstances. The next time insurmountable woes threaten to bury you, look up to heaven and say, "Lord, things down here look pretty bad right now, but I am rejoicing in You, and You just do what You think is best." Satan tempts Christians not to rejoice in their God during such times. By rejoicing in dire situations, we demonstrate that we actually trust God with the big picture, and we declare to those watching Who is in control and Who will resolve the matter. Rejoicing demonstrates faith without constraining God to our preconceived solutions (We don't try to squeeze God into our mode of operation.). So let us "rejoice evermore."

> I cannot choose to be strong, but I can choose to be joyful. And when I am willing to do that, strength will follow.
>
> Tim Hansel

> Happiness depends on what happens; joy does not.
>
> Oswald Chambers

The Prayerful Frame (v. 17)

"Pray without ceasing" does not mean we must constantly be uttering prayers. The Greek word *adialeiptos* is employed here which means "constantly recurring" not "continuously occurring." It would be impossible to pray 24 hours, a day seven days a week. But it is possible to have an active recurring prayer life. Perhaps the following illustration will help. Have you ever heard someone say after returning from a long road trip in which they were traveling with another person, "We talked the whole way home?" There were likely pauses in their conversation, but yet the dialogue was so enriching that they never sensed diminished fellowship. To "pray without ceasing" means to stay in contact with God in such a way that our praying is like a long conversation with short pauses – we never sense a break in conversation. The believer should pray at regular times and as exercised when needs arise (to confess sin, to make intercession, to seek grace in a time of need). The Lord should never be far from your thoughts at any time during the day.

> *LORD, Thou hast heard the desire of the humble: Thou wilt prepare their heart, Thou wilt cause thine ear to heart* (Ps. 10:17).

The Lord knows the desire of our hearts and grants the humble that desire. For what desire did the heart of the early church beat? Paul prayed for the souls of the nation of Israel – that they might be saved (Rom. 9:1-3, 10:1)! Paul also informed the Gentiles that they came to Christ as a result of God answering the prayers of Jewish Christians (2 Cor. 9:14). As discussed earlier, the early church prayed for boldness to spread the gospel message (Acts 4:24-30). How did the Lord answer their prayers?

> *And when they had prayed, the place was shaken where they were assembled together; and they were all filled with the Holy Ghost, and they spoke the word of God with boldness* (Acts 4:31).

Obviously, the Lord answered their prayers, and many souls were saved and added to the church. The longest prayer in the Bible, the Lord's prayer of John 17, reveals the heart of God for lost souls, for the preservation of the saved, and for unity of the church. It would seem that these matters ought to be at the forefront of our praying as well. Often we use prayer in a defensive posture – responding to personal needs, sickness, and the loss of a job. We certainly ought to solicit God on such matters, but let us not neglect the Great Commission – we need to charge forward against the gates of hell (Matt. 16:18). The church should be praying "offensively" for boldness, for opportunities to share the gospel, for the salvation of souls, for the protection of missionaries, and for fruitfulness in evangelical outreach. The New Testament Church spent their time praying for boldness and for those being persecuted because of their boldness (Acts 12:5; Phil. 1:19). Incidentally, Watchman Nee, martyred in China in 1972, referred to prayer as a weapon for which there is no defense. He said, "Prayer can do anything that God can do."[7]

Hudson Taylor, who also labored for the kingdom in China, had three important principles concerning prayer:

1. You can work without praying, but it is a bad plan.
2. You cannot pray in earnest without working.
3. Do not be so busy with work for Christ that you have no strength left for praying. True praying requires strength.[8]

When Charles Spurgeon was asked for the secret of his life and ministry in one sentence, this was his reply: "The prayers of my mother and the prayers of my church; this is the explanation of the life that I have lived in the world." St. Augustine said, "Pray as though everything depended on God, and work as though everything depended on you." Warren Wiersbe writes, "Prayer is not an escape from responsibility; it is our *response* to God's *ability*. True prayer energizes us for service and battle."[9]

As a Spiritual Weapon: Use "prayer" as an <u>offensive weapon</u> to defeat Satan through the proclamation of the gospel, the saving of souls, and the preservation of those laboring in this work. The great Napoleon once said, "The only way to have a conquering army is to have an army that is always fighting."[10] Labor in prayer, and preach the gospel.

The Thankful Frame (v. 18)

"In everything give thanks" – not "for" everything, but "in" everything. Why are we to give thanks in every situation? *"And we know that all things work together for good to them that love God, to them who are the called according to His purpose"* (Rom. 8:28) – meaning that we have exactly what the Lord wants us to have in order to live. Does a critical spirit strangle your mind from thinking positively? That is, do you see a half-empty glass of water or a half-full glass? The reality has not changed, but your perception of it has. Do the blooms of the rose bush or its thorns capture your attention? A thankful and critical mind frame cannot exist together.

There is always something to be thankful for if one is in a frame of mind to look for it. When the antique vase accidentally slips from your hands and shatters into a thousand pieces upon impact with the floor, praise the Lord it did not hit your foot. If you are involved with a traffic accident in which your vehicle is ruled a total wreck, praise the Lord you were kept safe. A thankful mind frame will always find something to praise God about, no matter how mentally stretching the trial is.

Hudson Taylor devoted his life to being a missionary in China through the heart of the 19th century. His vision for evangelism established the China Inland Mission, which successfully solicited thousands of missionaries to venture to China while he coordinated their activities. Tens of thousands of souls were saved.

The years in China were difficult for Taylor, but the fruitfulness of his labor is evident to this day. The fiery trials brought fresh realization that he was just a vessel in the Lord's hands to be used as His master saw fit. Diseases had claimed the lives of two the Taylors' children. Hudson and his wife Maria sent their remaining four children back to England with a trusted friend to be schooled and kept safe. Shortly after this,

Maria Taylor gave birth to a fifth son, but within a week, cholera took this child's life also. Soon after this his beloved wife became very ill. Hudson came to the bed of his 33-year-old wife, and said, "My darling, do you know that you are dying?" "Can it be so? I feel no pain, only weariness," was her reply. "Yes, you are going home. You will soon be with Jesus." His dying wife then apologized for leaving him alone in such difficult times.

Mrs. Duncan, an eyewitness of Mrs. Taylor's homegoing, later wrote of the event:

> I never witnessed such a scene. As dear Mrs. Taylor was breathing her last, Mr. Taylor knelt down – his heart so full – and committed her to the Lord; **thanking Him** for having given her and for the twelve and a half years of happiness they had had together; **thanking Him**, too, for taking her to His own blessed presence, and solemnly dedicating himself anew to His service.[11]

Three of his seven children dead, the other four in England and now his beloved wife home with Lord – Hudson wrote:

> From my inmost soul I delight in the knowledge that God does or deliberately permits all things and causes all things to work together for good to those who love Him (Rom. 8:28). ... I saw that **it was good** for the Lord to take her, **good indeed for her**, and in His love He took her painlessly; and **not less good for me** who must henceforth toil and suffer alone –yet not alone, for God is nearer to me than ever. And now I have to tell Him all my sorrows and difficulties, as I used to tell dear Maria.[12]

Shortly after this great trial of faith Hudson wrote to Mrs. Berger, "No language can express what He has been and is to me. Never does He leave me; constantly does He cheer me with

His love."[13] Hudson focused his mind on the good that God was accomplishing through the trial and thus could be thankful. The result of which was a closer fellowship with the Savior and a sanctified vessel for His use.

Thanksgiving and contentment are closely related. Paul informs the Christians at Philippi of what he had learned about contentment and thankfulness:

> *...I have learned, in <u>whatsoever state I am, therewith to be content</u>. I know both how to be abased, and I know how to abound: every where and in all things I am instructed both to be full and to be hungry, both to abound and to suffer need. I can do all things through Christ who strengtheneth me* (Phil. 4:11-13).

Paul instructed Timothy, *"But godliness with contentment is great gain ... having food and raiment let us be therewith content"* (1 Tim. 6:6-8). Verse 10 of that chapter speaks of those who were not content and thankful for what God had provided. They coveted money and erred from the faith. If God wanted us to have more than what we have, He would have bestowed it upon us. Being thankful defeats dissatisfaction.

The root of sin seems to be dissatisfaction, with selfishness and pride trailing close behind. When we are not content with what we have, we murmur against God. Murmuring is half-uttered complaints that God hears anyway. It results from looking backwards instead of Godward. The nation of Israel grumbled and complained the whole time they were in the Sinai Peninsula. Why? Because they were always comparing what they presently had to what they once had in Egypt – in slavery!

> *And the whole congregation **of the children of Israel murmured against Moses and Aaron in the wilderness**: And the children of Israel said unto them, Would to God*

*we had died by the hand of the LORD in the **land of Egypt**, when we sat by the flesh pots, and when we did eat bread to the full; for ye have brought us forth into this wilderness, to kill this whole assembly with hunger* (Ex. 16:2-3).

*And the people thirsted there for water; **and the people murmured against Moses**, and said, Wherefore is this that thou hast brought us up out of **Egypt**, to kill us and our children and our cattle with thirst* (Ex. 17:3)?

We complain and grumble today because our expectations were not met in comparison to what we had the month before. Last month we complained because again our expectations were not satisfied compared to the previous month. Looking backwards at what once was and comparing it to our wanton expectations leads to complaining. The spiritual response to all of our life's situations is to look for the good, to be thankful in all things, and to cease peering into history and comparing what was or what somebody else has.

Every good gift and every perfect gift is from above, and comes down from the Father of lights, with whom there is no variation or shadow of turning (Jas. 1:17).

As a Spiritual Weapon: Use "thanksgiving" to defeat dissatisfaction. This demonstrates faith in our God to handle the entire situation and to provide for all our needs. As God is seeking to develop the character of His children, a genuine thankful spirit during stressful situations may bring a more expedient end to the trial.

The Spiritual Frame (v. 19)

"Quench not the Spirit" – sin quenches and grieves the Holy Spirit (Eph. 4:30). Because the verb is in the present imperative tense, the phrase could easily be translated "stop quenching the Spirit." Wuest's Expanded Translation reads, "Stop stifling and suppressing the Spirit"! The Holy Spirit is likened to a flame (Isa. 4:4; Matt. 3:11; Rev. 4:5). He warms our hearts, enlightens our minds, and empowers the believer's spirit, but He can be resisted. It is the effectual working of the Holy Spirit that Paul warned against hindering or even snuffing out. Although the Holy Spirit is always present in the believer, when the believer chooses to sin, it is as if he or she had thrown a wet blanket over His energizing capacity. When an individual trusts Christ as his or her personal Savior, the Holy Spirit responds by regenerating that person (Tit. 3:5; Jn. 3:3-6). That new believer becomes an available tool in the hands of Almighty God to fill and pour out of as He chooses. But the extent that this is possible depends upon the personal sanctification of the believer.

> *But in a great house there are not only vessels of gold and of silver, but also of wood and of earth; and some to honor, and some to dishonor. If a man therefore purge himself from these, he shall be a vessel unto honor, sanctified, and meet for the master's use, and prepared unto every good work. Flee also youthful lusts: but follow righteousness, faith, charity, peace, with them that call on the Lord out of a pure heart* (2 Tim. 2:20-22).

As the believer submits to the known will of God, the Holy Spirit responds by filling that individual and equipping him or her for service with divine power. This can be clearly seen from the dawning days of the church age (Acts 1:4 with 1:12, and 2:1-4; Acts 4:23-32; Acts 6:9-10 with 7:55; Acts 9:6 with 9:17).

Submission leads to Spirit filling, which results in usefulness and fruitfulness. Thus, the believer is commanded to "be filled with the Holy Spirit" (Eph. 5:18). Paul informs us in Romans 6 that as we *know* and personally *yield* to truth we *present* our bodies to God as a living sacrifice. We enable the Holy Spirit by losing ourselves through submission and yielding ourselves to God's revealed truth.

Paul declares to Timothy that, when we make the choice to flee ungodliness, we become vessels of honor available for God's sovereign use (2 Tim. 2:20). According to God's fore-knowledge of both our failures and our obedience, He has pre-ordained us to specific works to accomplish. This is why Peter exhorts Christians to *"make your election sure,"* and Paul instructs them to *"walk in the works that God has foreordained."* We must truly lose our life to gain the vitality God desires for our spiritual life in Him (Lk. 9:24). It is only by the empowerment of the Holy Spirit that our testimony can shine forth Christ (Zech. 4:6).

> A holy life will produce the deepest impression. Lighthouses blow no horns; they only shine.
>
> D. L. Moody

As a Spiritual Weapon: We are equipped to oppose the enemy when we keep a spiritual mindset (forsake and confess sin). Spirit filling occurs as a sovereign act of God based on our obedience and submission to His revealed will.

The Teachable Frame (v. 20)

"Despise not prophesyings" – to despise prophesy (God's declared Word) would keep the Holy Spirit from aiding our

worship and from producing personal spiritual growth. Before the Scripture was supplied to us through the apostles, there were prophets who immediately declared the Word of God to the local body. What is in view is the neglect of studying, understanding, meditating on and memorizing God's Word. It is extremely important for younger and older Christians to be studying the Word of God. Peter instructs, *"As newborn babes, desire the sincere milk of the word, that ye may grow thereby"* (1 Pet. 2:2). Both Paul (1 Cor. 3:2) and the writer of Hebrews (Heb. 5:12-13) acknowledge the need to study the foundational truths of the Christian faith (the milk of the Word), as well as the necessity to move on to the more substantial teachings of the Bible.

What weapon did the Lord Jesus use to defeat satanic temptation? The Word of God – the sword of the Spirit. At the conclusion of His 40-day fast, the Lord Jesus directly quoted three passages from the book of Deuteronomy. In his solicitations to sin, Satan twisted and misquoted Psalm 91. John Darby once stated, "The devil is never more satanic than when he has a Bible in his hands." Why? Because there is no truth in him (Jn. 8:44). So the believer should not be amazed when the cults change and misquote Scripture to teach that Jesus Christ was not God in the flesh, or to refute the doctrine of the Trinity, or to deny that there is an eternal place of judgment called hell.

The Word of God is likened to a sharp sword, and in the book of Revelation, it clearly symbolizes the direct words of the Lord Jesus to execute judgment upon the wicked:

*And take the helmet of salvation, and **the sword of the Spirit, which is the word of God*** (Eph. 6:17).

*For the **word of God** is quick, and powerful, **and sharper than any two-edged sword**, piercing even to the dividing* *asunder of soul and spirit, and of the joints and marrow, and is a discerner of the thoughts and intents of the heart* (Heb. 4:12).

*And He had in his right hand seven stars: and **out of His mouth went a sharp two-edged sword**: and His countenance was as the sun shineth in His strength* (Rev. 1:16).

*Repent; or else I will come unto thee quickly, and will fight against them with **the sword of my mouth*** (Rev. 2:16).

The Word of God is both an offensive and a defensive spiritual weapon. As a defensive tool, it actively discerns our own thoughts (Heb. 4:12), sharpens our conscience, and aids in defeating the onset of temptation.

Let my heart be sound in Thy statutes; that I be not ashamed (Ps. 119:80).

Thy word have I hid in mine heart, that I might not sin against Thee (Ps. 119:11).

As an offensive weapon, truth aggressively assaults deception and false teaching. Paul told Titus that knowing the Word of God in order to oppose false doctrine in the church was a spiritual qualification for those in church leadership. *"Holding fast the faithful word as he hath been taught, that he may be able by sound doctrine both to exhort and to convince the gainsayers [opposers]"* (Titus 1:9). The Lord Jesus proclaimed, *"...know the truth and the truth will set you free"* (Jn. 8:32). Since divine truth is the only defense against Satan's lies and deceit, the unsaved have no defense against him. Corrie Ten Boom put it this way: "Satan wastes no ammunitions on those who are dead in trespasses and sins." So, dear believer, expect a confrontation when you start wielding the sword of truth – it provokes the enemy into conflict. If you prod unsaved souls with the Word of God and they laugh at you – just poke them again with the sword of truth. Sooner or later they will get the point.

The use of Scripture to express truth is absolutely critical in the work of evangelism. *"Faith cometh by hearing and hearing by the Word of God"* (Rom. 10:17). A believer should apply Scripture directly to questions asked by the unsaved and cite as little commentary as possible. In this manner, both the power of the Word of God and the Spirit of God are unleashed on the unsaved soul. We are often ineffective in evangelism because we get in God's way. We are mere vessels that He pours into and out of; He is the One energizing all the work that counts for eternity. The Lord Jesus used the technique of asking questions and appealing directly to Scripture when addressing the questions of a pugnacious lawyer (Lk. 10:25-26). Using the Bible in this fashion will keep you out of arguments. There is nothing to argue about; you have not said anything – God has said it all. By not interjecting commentary, you have not given the listener an escape for their frustration – they themselves know that the argument is with God.

As a Spiritual Weapon: Use God's Word to attack deception, rebuke false doctrine, and to affect unsaved souls. This will require hiding the Word of God in your heart.

The Judicial Frame (v. 21)
"Prove all things." This mind frame is linked with the teachable mind frame. The previous frame employs the Word

of God to work upon our own hearts, the unsaved, or in direct opposition to false doctrine. In the present culture, blatant wickedness besieges the heart of the rebel, and subtle deception snares the complacent believer. Deceit is often thoroughly forged with something acceptable. Consequently, much discernment is required in daily conduct, or the believer will certainly fall prey to the enemy's trickery and craftiness. New Age propaganda has infiltrated corporate America's human resource departments, the medical profession, government- operated schools, and entertainment. Many self-promoting preachers today are using the gospel for profit. The cults are advertising strong pro-family and pro-morality themes. They often ensnare individuals into their ranks by promoting good intentions at the cost of sound doctrine. Contemporary children's movies often disguise pantheism, animism, reincarnation, and necromancy within carefully arranged humor, special effects, and exhilarating music to create a more palatable message for children to digest under the eye of undiscerning Christian parents.

Concerning the matter of discerning holy truth from evil deception, Luke endorsed the behavior of the Bereans as a good example to follow. *"More noble ... they received the Word with all readiness of mind, and **searched the Scriptures daily**, whether those things were so"* (Acts 17:11). They were confronted with the gospel message and sought to verify or disprove it by investigating Old Testament Scripture. Similarly, every child of God should be like the Bereans, proving matters out to determine what is true and false. We should be discerning! Paul exhorted Timothy:

*Study to show thyself approved unto God, a workman that needeth not to be ashamed, **rightly dividing the word of truth**. But shun profane and vain babblings: for* *they will increase unto more ungodliness* (2 Tim. 2:15-16).

John instructed the believers, *"Believe not every spirit* [teacher], *but test the spirits whether they are of God"* (1 Jn. 4:1-4). He also informed them of an anointing that they had received at spiritual rebirth. There is no need to pray for this anointing; every believer already has it. It is always spoken of in the past tense and has the purpose of giving spiritual discernment concerning what is truth and what is false.

> *But **ye have an unction [anointing] from the Holy One, and ye know all things**. I have not written unto you because ye know not the truth, but because ye know it, and that no lie is of the truth* (1 Jn. 2:20-21).

> *These things have I written unto you concerning them that seduce you. **But the anointing which ye have received of Him abideth in you, and ye need not that any man teach you: but as the same anointing teacheth you of all things**, and is truth, and is no lie, and even as it hath taught you, ye shall abide in Him* (1 Jn. 2:26-27).

As A Spiritual Weapon: Use God's Word to validate what is truth and what is deception – to discern what is of God and what is a forgery. Slothfulness leads to embracing deception.

> *Thy word is a lamp unto my feet and a light unto my path* (Ps. 119:105).

The Consecrated Frame (v. 22)

"Abstain from the appearance of evil." This mind frame fully consecrates one's spirit, soul and body for God's purposes by abhorring evil in thought and deed. The matter hinges on the believer's understanding that who and what he or she was positionally in Adam is dead (Eph. 4:22; Rom. 6:6). All that we were before Christ is no more – we died with Him at Calvary. Because we have been legally declared dead, we may receive a new life – His life. We must now endeavor to live His life in practice and not follow our own ambitions.

> *For the love of Christ constraineth us; because we thus judge, that if one died for all, then were all dead: And that He died for all, that they which live should not henceforth live unto themselves, but unto Him which died for them, and rose again. Wherefore henceforth know we no man after the flesh: yea, though we have known Christ after the flesh, yet now henceforth know we Him no more. Therefore if any man be in Christ, he is a new creature: old things are passed away; behold, all things are become new* (2 Cor. 5:14-17).

From God's perspective, a believer commits spiritual adultery when he or she lives a carnal life in lieu of a crucified life. It angers the Lord and summons His chastening hand to execute discipline upon the believer. The Lord knows that we will be the most joyful and fruitful while remaining on the "straight and narrow" way.

> *Ye adulterers and adulteresses, know ye not that the friendship of the world is enmity with God? Whosoever therefore will be a friend of the world is the enemy of God. Do ye think that the Scripture saith in vain, The spirit that dwelleth in us lusteth to envy? But He giveth more grace. Wherefore He saith, God resisteth the proud, but giveth grace unto the humble. Submit yourselves therefore to God. Resist the devil, and he will flee*

from you. Draw nigh to God, and He will draw nigh to you. Cleanse your hands, ye sinners; and purify your hearts, ye double minded (Jam. 4:4-8).

Being blameless is mentioned first in a list of qualifications for the appointment of church leaders in both 1 Timothy and Titus (1 Tim. 3:2; Tit. 1:6). Blameless means "one's conduct is above reproach." It is a lifestyle that is so centered in holy living that no legitimate accusation of wrongdoing can be asserted. Being blameless means living a lifestyle that will not stumble a weaker brother in his faith (1 Cor. 8:9), or hinder the unsaved from hearing the gospel (1 Cor. 9:12), or bring reproach on the name of Christ (1 Tim. 3:7). Besides being blameless in conduct, the consecrated mind frame also dedicates the mind to God's use. The consecrated mind frame hinges on the believer's understanding that there is absolutely nothing in his or her flesh that can please God. Only when a believer's spirit, soul and body are yielded unto righteousness and the Holy Spirit's control can he or she be useful for the kingdom of God.

For I know that in me (that is, in my flesh), dwelleth no good thing: for to will is present with me; but how to perform that which is good I find not. For the good that I would I do not: but the evil which I would not, that I do (Rom. 7:18-19).

For the flesh lusteth against the Spirit, and the Spirit against the flesh: and these are contrary the one to the other: so that ye cannot do the things that ye would (Gal. 5:17).
And they that are Christ's have crucified the flesh with the affections and lusts. If we live in the Spirit, let us also walk in the Spirit (Gal. 5:24-25).

As one crucifies the lusts of the flesh, he or she then can yield up to the Lord their total being, including the mind. C. S. Lewis implores the believer, "Die before you die. There is no chance after." Oswald Chambers wrote, "It is the great moment of our lives when we decide that sin must die right out, not be curbed or suppressed or counteracted, but crucified." There is no room in our minds to think the way we did before coming to Christ. The consecrated mind frame does not allow the mind to pursue its own inherent vanity and lusts. It does not allow the mind to drift into the land of imagination to indulge the fallen nature. The believer must **remove** all unholy thinking, **renew** his or her mind to approve what is good and acceptable (This requires replacing what was removed.), and **resist** the temptation to return to "stinking thinking."

> *This I say therefore, and testify in the Lord, that ye henceforth walk not as other Gentiles walk, in the vanity of their mind* (Eph. 4:17).

> *And be **renewed in the spirit of your mind**; And that ye put on the new man, which after God is created in righteousness and true holiness* (Eph. 4:23-24).

> *Among whom also we all had our conversation in times past in the lusts of our flesh, fulfilling the **desires of the flesh and of the mind**; and were by nature the children of wrath, even as others* (Eph. 2:3).

Sanctification is not a heavy yoke, but a joyful liberation.

Corrie Ten Boom

As a Spiritual Weapon: Remember these three R's: Remove, Renew, and Resist. When the temptation to sin begins to sway your mind, be sure all strongholds in your heart are removed (This requires tearing down lies and false perceptions.), then renew your mind by replacing unwholesome thoughts with proper thinking (Phil. 4:8). Once your mind has been put into subjection to what God says, resist the devil by standing firm in the faith. In short, if evil takes shape in your mind, avoid and resist that evil.

Other Mind Frames

In addition to the ten mind frames explained above from 1 Thessalonians 5, the author would suggest two more important frames: recalling God's sovereignty and forgiveness.

The Recalling Frame

In the mental fitness chapter, we explored recalling God's past faithfulness to settle our minds when difficulties arise. As a mind frame, use "recalling" to bring to your mind the fact that God is sovereign over His creation. Remembering that God is sovereign over all will defeat feelings of jealousy and discontent. God is in control and everything is as He allows it. Nothing occurs in creation, including your trials, which does not first pass over His desk, so to speak. Paul found this mind frame to be the secret in learning contentment during periods of lack.

> *But I rejoiced in the Lord greatly, that now at the last your care of me hath flourished again; wherein ye were also careful, **but ye lacked opportunity**. Not that I speak in respect of want: **for I have learned, in whatsoever state I am, therewith to be content**. I know both how to*

*be abased, and I know how to abound: every where and in all things I am instructed both to be full and to be hungry, both to abound and to suffer need. **I can do all things through Christ which strengtheneth me*** (Phil. 4:10-13).

Right this very moment you have exactly as much money as God wants you to have. If He wanted you to have more, your bank account would show it. The reason He has not bestowed more monetary blessings in your direction is that you don't need it, or you would be a poor steward of it, or He is teaching you lessons concerning budgeting and giving. The Lord knows what He is doing, and His doings serve our best *interest*. So let us appreciate what we have, assess our present condition with a spiritual mindset, adjust where we lack, and accept everything as from the Lord. Let us learn contentment.

This mind frame will keep bents of coveting and unrighteous jealousy in check. King Saul, even after understanding that the kingdom had been promised to David, was lifted up in pride and jealousy. Saul could not accept God's sovereign rule or the just punishment he received for his own blundering mistakes. If we understand that we have exactly what God desires us to possess and our neighbors have exactly what God bestows upon them, what room is there for envy and coveting in our thinking?

What is your mind's capability to recall? My capacity seems to be decreasing with each passing day. Isaac Asimov writes:

> The memory capacity of even an ordinary human mind is fabulous. We may not consider ourselves particularly adept at remembering technical data ... but consider how many faces we can recognize, how many names call up some past incident, how many words we can spell and

define ... It is estimated that in a lifetime, a brain can store one million billion "bits" of information.[14]

With so much God-given ability to store away information, let us endeavor to recall God's goodness and faithfulness. Focusing our thoughts upon all His ways, which are past finding out, will certainly aid our minds to remember that God is a good God. *"Thou art good and does good"* (Ps. 119:68).

As a Spiritual Weapon. Use the mind frame of recalling God's sovereignty to defeat thoughts of envy and coveting.

The Forgiving Frame

Bitterness is defeated by forgiveness. Bitterness is truly a self-imposed affliction that literally "presses down on the heart." Bitterness plagues the church and affects every relationship the bitter individual has, including open fellowship with the Lord. If we realize that others will naturally hurt us, it is only reasonable that we must develop a forgiving heart in order to interact with each other. Certainly, the children of God, our friends, and even the unsaved are not our enemies; therefore, we must learn to forgive them, or we impose an adversarial disposition on the relationship.

Watchman Nee understood this matter; "Aside from Satan, the Lord has no enemies, only potential friends." He also said, "If we have died and indeed we have in Christ it should be impossible to be offended." Early in his Christian walk, Watchman realized his evangelistic ministry had been stifled because he had offended others and not asked for their forgiveness so he created a list of those he had potentially offended and apologized to each one. Immediately after this, he witnessed dozens of souls won to Christ.[15] Bitterness stifles the Spirit of God from working in our lives.

There are primarily two Greek words in the New Testament that are translated "forgive." *Aphiemi* (af-ee'-ay-mee) is the most common and may also be translated "leave," "suffer," "give," "sent away," "yield up," or "put away." *Aphiemi* is associated with the act of forgiving 48 times in the New Testament, but oddly it is only employed four times in all the epistles to speak of forgiveness. *Aphiemi* primarily means "to send forth" or "to send away" (*apo*, "from," *hiemi*, "to send") or by implication "to forgive." It views God's willful action of sending away the remembrance of our sin as illustrated in Psalm 103:12; *"As far as the east is from the west, so far hath He removed our transgressions from us."* Or in Hebrews 10:17; *"Their sins and iniquities will I remember no more."* We must realize that it is humanly possible to forgive and not forget, and to forget and not forgive; therefore, forgetting is not forgiving. This aspect of forgiving declares that the wrong has been put away and will not be remembered any more.

The second Greek word used to speak of forgiveness in the New Testament is *charizomai* (khar-id'-zom-ahee) which means, "to bestow a favor unconditionally or to freely give or release." Interestingly, 14 of the 24 times *charizomai* is found in the New Testament it is translated as some variation of "forgive." Even more fascinating is that 12 of these 14 occurrences are located in the Epistles. The only two occurrences of *charizomai* in the Gospel accounts are found together in one parable (Luke 7). Paul explains the motive for "releasing" another from the desire for vengeance and retribution.

> *Forbearing one another, and forgiving one another, if any man have a quarrel against any:* **even as Christ forgave you, so also do ye**" (Col. 3:13).

*And be ye kind one to another, tenderhearted, forgiving one another, **even as God for Christ's sake hath for-given you**"* (Eph. 4:32).

How do these two different words relate to the activity of forgiving each other? The mechanics of forgiveness (how to send away offenses) seems to be associated with the word *aphiemi*, while *charizomai* addresses the motive for releasing the offender with an unconditional attitude. The "how to's" include going privately to a brother who has offended you (Matt. 18:15), or to a brother who has been offended by you (Matt. 5:23-24) to seek resolution. If there is acknowledgement of the sin, a declaration of forgiveness should then follow the offending party's confession and repentance. We must be willing to repeatedly declare forgiveness to those who repent of the offense (Matt. 18:21-22). General Oglethorpe said to John Wesley, "I never forgive!," to which Wesley replied, "Then, sir, I hope you never sin."[16] The fact is that we do sin and that we need the forgiveness of others and of the Lord Jesus. Let us not withhold from others what we have freely received.

Why are the mechanics of forgiveness spoken of in the Gospel accounts, but the motive to forgive found in the Epistles? Because prior to Calvary the motive to forgive (Christ's suffering for our sin that we might be forgiven) was not evident. This is why *aphiemi* is predominantly applied in the Gospels and *charizomai* is found in the Epistles. *Aphiemi* speaks of the process and mindset of forgiveness, while *charizomai* implores us "to freely release" in light of what we have been forgiven.

So how does the forgiving mind frame work? As soon as you have been offended, the believer must "freely release" all self-right to exact vengeance and to get even. Whatever the matter, it is less painful and distasteful than the Lord Jesus bearing our sin under divine judgment. So you deliver the matter to the Lord to resolve. "Dearly beloved, avenge not yourselves, but rather give place unto wrath: for it is written, Vengeance is Mine; I will repay, saith the Lord" (Rom. 12:19). Then, when you have control of your emotions, the guilty party should be confronted. If he repents, you have won a brother, and you should verbally declare forgiveness to him (2 Cor. 2:7-8). If he does not repent, you don't seize the situation back from the Lord, for you have released it to Him as a sweet smelling sacrifice (1 Pet. 2:19-20). Releasing means it will not affect the "foreground" of your daily affairs; it remains in the "background" of your thinking so that when the offending party does repent you are quite willing and ready to declare forgiveness. It is unbiblical to declare forgiveness to someone without them first acknowledging their behavior as wrong. To declare forgiveness to an offending party prior to them admitting their sin is an affront to God's righteousness and serves only to promote a continuance of sin.

If what they are saying about you is true, mend your ways. If it isn't true, forget it, and go on and serve the Lord.

H. A. Ironside

The sandal-tree perfumes when riven the ax that laid it low;
Let man, who hopes to be forgiven, forgive and bless his foe.

Sadi

As a Spiritual Weapon. Use forgiveness to prevent your heart from hardening under the pressure of bitterness. Release offenses to the Lord immediately, and declare forgiveness to those who offend you after they have confessed the wrong as sin. This mind frame provides a "jail break" for those believers who have imprisoned themselves through a spirit of unforgiveness.

Summary of Mind Frames and Spiritual Benefits

Mind Frame	When to Use	Spiritual Benefit
Love	For people problems	Christ's love is witnessed – hard hearts are softened.
Faith	When action is required	Reviewing God's past faithfulness defeats doubts, and aids others to trust.
Hope	When joy has diminished	Reviewing God's promises defeats discouragement, and depression, joy results.
Rejoice	When facing trials	God affects miracles for His glory.
Prayer	For gospel offensive	Saints are made bold to preach with power.
Thanksgiving	In all circumstances	Defeats dissatisfaction, and brings contentment.
Spiritual	In matters of sin	Divine fellowship restored, available for Spirit filling.
Teachable	For learning sound doctrine	Truth defeats the enemy's deception (darkness).
Discerning	In questionable behavior	Defeats trickery – validates what is wise and godly.
Consecrated	For temptations to sin	Eliminates mind strongholds, and purifies the whole man.
Recalling	Questioning God's wisdom	Defeats thoughts of envy and discontentment.
Forgiving	When offended and hurt	Defeats bitterness – releases the mind to focus/serve.

A Mind Set upon Christ

Paul realized that the best means of preventing the Colossian believers from slipping into the deceit of intellectualism or the pitfalls of legalism was to set their minds upon the Lord Jesus. His epistle to the Colossians establishes Christ's supremacy over all creation for He is the omnipotent Creator and Sustainer, the Savior of mankind, and Lord over all. Because all the fullness of the Godhead bodily dwells in Christ (Col. 2:9), Christ alone is the source of knowledge, wisdom, peace, grace, and access to the Father. Paul repeatedly reminds the Colossian believers of their blessed union with Christ in chapter 2; because they were one "with Christ," they were complete "in Him." In chapter 3, Paul submits that our very identification with Christ should exhort us to holy living. The believer's *position* in Christ should motivate his or her *practice*.

> *If ye then be risen **with Christ, seek those things which are above**, where Christ sitteth on the right hand of God. **Set your affection on things above**, not on things on the earth. For ye are dead, and your life is hid **with Christ** in God. When Christ, who is our life, shall appear, then shall ye also appear with Him in glory. Mortify therefore your members which are upon the earth; fornication, uncleanness, inordinate affection, evil concupiscence, and covetousness, which is idolatry* (Col. 3:1-5).

The Holy Text intertwines what God has done in Christ and what we should do in Christ. Salvation is God's doing, but living out our salvation is our responsibility made possible by God's grace. Through spiritual birth, we are made one **with Christ** – an eternal union held together by God Himself. Notice the key to proper devotion on our part: "Set your affection on things above." Not affections, but affection. We are to only have **one affection** and that is Christ. To please Him and exalt Him is our sole purpose in life. Yet, it is so easy to be distracted by things and allow this one affection to be displaced. D. L. Moody understood the importance of the believer's occupation with Christ rather than with that which opposes Christ.

> In 1893, the World's Columbian Exposition was held in Chicago, and more than 21 million people visited the exhibits. Among the features was a "World Parliament of Religions," with representatives of the world's religions, meeting to share their "best points" and perhaps come up with a new religion for the world. Evangelist D. L. Moody saw this as a great opportunity for evangelism. He used churches, rented theaters, and even rented a circus tent (when the show was not on) to present the gospel of Jesus Christ. His friends wanted Moody to attack the "Parliament of Religions," but he refused. "I am going to make Jesus Christ so attractive," he said, "that men will turn to Him." Moody knew that Jesus Christ was the preeminent Saviour, not just one of many "religious leaders" of history. The "Chicago Campaign" of 1893 was probably the greatest evangelistic endeavor in D. L. Moody's life, and thousands came to Christ.[1]

Moody had a choice: attack hordes of religious people visiting Chicago or extol the glorious Savior through his preaching for all to see. He chose to exalt Christ, and thousands fell in love with the same altogether lovely One that Moody cherished. The soul who is in love with Jesus Christ inescapably will be a good evangelist! This individual knows the peace of God and wants to share it with others.

The Lord Jesus not only made **peace with** God, but now offers us the **peace of** God. He not only offers salvation of the soul, but of the mind as well. *"Therefore, being justified by faith, we have **peace with God** through our Lord Jesus Christ"* (Rom. 5:1). *"And the **peace of God**, which passeth all understanding, shall keep your hearts, and minds through Christ Jesus"* (Phil. 4:7).

The Greek word translated "peace" is *eirene* (i-ray'-nay). It is derived from a verb meaning to "bond together." It literally means to "be made at one again," which is reflected in Acts 7:26 when Moses sought to make two quarreling *brothers "at one again."* In the RV *eirene* is translated "peace" 90 out of 91 times, the only exception being Acts 7:26. In the AV *eirene* is translated peace all but three times. The outstanding references being to "rest," "quietness," and "at one again." Applying the meaning of this word to Romans 5:1 then means that we are "one again" with God when we believe the gospel message, this is the saving of the soul. However, Philippians 4:7 refers to the saving of the mind – it is achieved when we are "one again" with Christ in thinking, affections, and attitudes.

The Lord Jesus understood the significance of being one with Him in salvation and in thinking. Notice His first conversation with His disciples on Resurrection day:

> *Then the same day at evening, being the first day of the week, when the doors were shut where the disciples were assembled for fear of the Jews, came Jesus and stood in the midst, and saith unto them, **Peace be unto you**. And when He had so said, He showed unto them His hands*

> *and His side. Then were the disciples glad, when they*
> *saw the Lord. Then said Jesus to them again, **Peace be***
> ***unto you**: as My Father hath sent Me, even so send I you*
> (Jn. 20:19-21).

Why did the Lord say to His disciples "Peace be unto you" twice? Wouldn't once have been sufficient? At Christ's initial appearing, we find the disciples discouraged and fearful. The Lord knew that His apostles needed to have peace within before they could convey a message of peace outwardly. Once the disciples had been with the Lord, literally one with Him again, their hearts were made glad – there was peace within. Now, the Lord could send them out to preach a message of peace to others. It is impossible to convey peace to others unless the believer has laid hold of the peace of God. Being one again with Christ brings peace to the soul. Whenever a believer is not at peace, he should ask himself, "In what area of my life am I not one with Christ?" Certainly *"looking unto Jesus, the author and finisher of our faith"* (Heb. 12:2) should be the captivating goal of the believer. In fact, it is only by looking unto Jesus that the non-believer can obtain peace as well.

On January 6, 1850, a snowstorm almost crippled the city of Colchester, England; and a teenage boy was unable to get to the church he usually attended. So he made his way to a nearby Primitive Methodist chapel, where an ill-prepared [man] was substituting for the absent preacher. His text was Isaiah 45:22 – *"Look unto Me, and be ye saved, all the ends of the earth."* For many months this young teenager had been miserable and under deep conviction; but though he had been reared in church (both his father and grandfather were preachers), he did not have the assurance of salvation. The unprepared substitute minister did not have much to say, so he kept repeating the text. "A man need not go to college to learn to look," he shouted. "Anyone can look—a child can look!" About that time, he saw the visitor sitting to one side, and he pointed at him and said, "Young man, you look very miserable. Young man, look to Jesus Christ!" The young man did look by faith, and that was how the great preacher Charles Haddon Spurgeon was converted.[2]

For the unsaved, the difference between perishing and living and between condemnation and salvation is looking unto Jesus Christ by faith. For the saved, the difference between an existence of anxiety and a life of peace is continuing to look to Him by faith. As we become one with Him and trust Him, His peace becomes a reality in daily living.

> *These things I have spoken unto you, **that in Me ye might have peace**. In the world ye shall have tribulation: but be of good cheer; I have overcome the world* (Jn. 16:33).

> *Take My yoke upon you, and **learn of Me**; for I am meek and lowly in heart, and ye* shall **find rest unto your souls** (Matt. 11:29).

The Lord's peace comes to us as we look to and learn of Him. As we learn of Him (His mind, His character, His love, etc.), we become one with Him. Oneness with the Savior brings peace into our lives. This peaceful realization came to Hudson Taylor after a strenuous time of missionary ministry in China. He wrote of his discovery to his dear sister McCarthy:

> *"If we believe not ... He abideth faithful"* (2 Tim. 2:13). I looked to Jesus and saw (and when I saw, oh how joy flowed!). He has said, *"I will never leave you"* (Heb.

13:5). Ah, there is rest! I thought. "I have been striving in vain to rest in Him. I'll strive no more. For He has promised to abide with me – never to leave me, never to fail me." ... The sweetest part, if one may speak of one part being sweeter than another, **is the rest which full identification with Christ brings.** I am no longer anxious about anything, as I realized this; for He, I know, is able to carry out His will, and His will is mine. It makes no matter where He places me, or how. That is rather for Him to consider than for me; for in the easiest positions He must give me His grace, and in the most difficult His grace is sufficient."[3]

Dear believer, if you are not at peace within, there is some area of your life that you are not one with Him. You must set your mind again upon Him. Perhaps it is an issue of forgiveness, or lowliness, or compassion, or in truth, or in submission to authority. Seek to "be at one again," and His peace will flood your soul. Find rest for your soul by walking in the good way (Jer. 6:16).

The moment you wake up each morning all your wishes and hopes for the day rush at you like wild animals. And the first job of each morning consists in shoving them all back; in listening to that other voice, taking that other point of view, letting that other, larger, stronger, quieter life come flowing in.

C. S. Lewis

The Blessed Mind of Christ

No study on the mind would be complete without highlighting the Lord's ultimate desire for all believers – that we obtain His mind. Paul exhorts the believers at Philippi to *"be like-minded, having the same love, being of one accord, of one mind"* (Phil. 2:2). How is it possible for believers from different cultural and ethnic backgrounds, with unique problems and difficulties, to have one mind? The answer is revealed, *"Let this mind be in you, which was also in Christ Jesus"* (Phil. 2:5). When all believers have the lowly mind of Christ, we will be of one mind. It is a mindset that is not puffed up in vain glory, but is focused on the needs of others. Christ was the Servant of servants before He was the King of kings. Let this mind be in you.

The early church seems to have enjoyed one mindedness. *"And the multitude of them that believed were of **one heart** and of **one soul**: neither said any of them that ought of the things which he possessed was his own; but they had all things common"* (Acts 4:32). Only when believers have surrendered their minds, hearts, and souls – yes, all that defines them as a living person – will there be complete unity in the body of Christ. For His Body, the Church, should not be composed of foreign objects that adversely affect its divine operation through individual and selfish ambitions. God has revealed to us by the essence of Himself that where godliness resides, individuality and unity will also exist in complete harmony.

In the last chapter, we acknowledged the sweet internal peace that captivates the believer's soul when he or she is one with Christ in thinking and character. How is a local church affected when all in fellowship become thoroughly unified with Christ? Clearly, the early church obtained this unification with Christ; the consequences of which are still apparent unto this day. Note the numerous acknowledgments of church unity and the miraculous evangelical results.

First Example

"These all continued with one accord in prayer and supplication ..." (Acts 1:14).

"When the day of Pentecost was fully come, they were all with one accord in one place ..." (Acts 2:1).

Result: Spirit filling (Acts 2:4), and 3000 souls are saved (Acts 2:41).

Second Example

"They continuing daily with one accord ..." (Acts 2:46).

Result: *"The Lord added to the church daily..."* (Acts 2:47).

Third Example

"Now Peter and John went up together into the temple ..." (Acts 3:1).

Result: A lame man was healed (Acts 3:8), and about 5000 souls were saved (Acts 4:4).

Fourth Example

"... they lifted up their voice to God with one accord ..." (Acts 4:24).

"... those that believed were of one heart and of one soul ..." (Acts 4:32).

Result: *"...all were filled with the Holy Spirit, and they spoke the word of God with boldness"* (Acts 4:31).

Fifth Example

"... they were all with one accord in Solomon's porch" (Acts 5:12).

Result: *"And believers were the more added to the Lord, multitudes both of men and women ..."* (Acts 5:14).

Sixth Example

"And daily in the temple, and in every house, they ceased not to teach and preach Jesus Christ" (Acts 5:42).

Result: *"And in those days, when the number of the disciples was multiplied"* (Acts 6:1).

Seventh Example

"... there arose murmuring of the Grecians against the Hebrews, because their widows were neglected ..." (Acts. 6:1).

Note: For the first time, there is disunity, and the work of evangelism is hindered.

Result: After the apostles gave direction to the Christian assembly (Chose deacons to be in charge of the ministry to widows), which effectively resolved the problem, we read, *"The saying pleased the whole multitude"* (Acts 6:5). As a result of obtaining one mindedness again, *"The word of God increased, and the number of the disciples multiplied in Jerusalem greatly"* (Acts 6:7).

In summary, the early church was successful in evangelism when there was unity and Christ-mindedness among the disciples. When there were division and factions in the church, their testimony was marred, the Spirit quenched, and fruitfulness ceased. The lesson for us all – lay hold of the mind of Christ. This will bring unity to the church, which will then have only one goal: "that all things be unto the glory of God." On the eve of His suffering, the Lord acknowledged by His prayer the inseparable link between unity and displaying the glory of God. *"And the glory which Thou gavest Me. I have given them, that they may be one, even as We are one"* (Jn. 17:22). When the Church is unified, the glory of God is displayed, and the unsaved are won to Christ!

Thus, it is sometimes appropriate that brethren work separately that the glory of God be manifested and the work of God not be hindered. Anthony Norris Groves departed from a lucrative dental profession to be a missionary to India in the 1830's. Mr. and Mrs. A. N. Groves distributed their wealth among the needy in England and proceeded to India – trusting all their provisions to the Lord. G. H. Lang wrote in Groves' biography, *Anthony Norris Groves,* about Groves' passion for gospel ministry and the needful unity among God's laborers to accomplish it:

… when dissension arises between workers, they must either part, as did Barnabas and Paul, or the work withers at its roots. But spiritual union is spiritual strength."[1]

On this side of glorification, brethren will not always agree. Yet, after Christ's coming for His church, we have the glorious promise that all the brethren *will come into unity* (Eph. 4:13). Until then, let us be unified in the whole or be separately unified in part, that the great commission continue without omission. When you obtain the mind of Christ, you will be able to pray that your critics further the gospel of Christ also. Paul was able to rejoice in the gospel ministry of his critics, though they slandered him while preaching (Phil. 1:17). Why? Because they were *preaching Christ*! Warren Wiersbe relates a more modern day example of this selfless attitude of the mind of Christ.

It is a matter of historic record that the two great English evangelists, John Wesley and George Whitefield, disagreed on doctrinal matters. Both of them were very successful, preaching to thousands of people and seeing multitudes come to Christ. It is reported that somebody asked Wesley if he expected to see Whitefield in heaven, and the evangelist replied, "No, I do not."

"Then you do not think Whitefield is a converted man?" "Of course he is a converted man!" Wesley said. "But I do not expect to see him in heaven—because he will be so close to the throne of God and I so far away that I will not be able to see him!" Though he differed with his brother in some matters, Wesley did not have any envy in his heart, nor did he seek to oppose Whitefield's ministry.[2]

Mind Frames

We wonder at Thy lowly mind,
And fain would like Thee be,
And all our rest and pleasure fine,
In learning, Lord, of Thee.

James G. Deck

One Goal – Christlikeness

... Now the body is not for fornication, but for the Lord; and the Lord for the body (1 Cor. 6:13).

What? know ye not that your body is the temple of the Holy Ghost which is in you, which ye have of God, and ye are not your own? For ye are bought with a price: therefore glorify God in your body, and in your spirit, which are God's (1 Cor. 6:19-20).

It is imperative that believers understand that their body, soul, and spirit have been redeemed by the blood of Jesus Christ and are Christ's purchased possessions. Not only did the Lord save the believer's soul and spirit, but also the body – "the body is for the Lord and the Lord for the body." The Christian's only goal in life is to give the Creator honor and glory through complete submission to His will. To achieve this goal, the believer must be liberated from all controlling hindrances. In this way, our God has a visible means to express His lovingkindness from heavenly realms into an evil and cursed world. We are truly His light upon a dismal planet (Matt. 5:14).

The six mind exercises presented in this book are not for the purpose of increasing intellectual power or stirring up natural resolve or inherent abilities to serve God. This would be foolish and only add to the tendency of an individual to pursue God through natural abilities. The ultimate goal of these mind exercises is to obtain a fortified mind against internal or external aggression. This mind will be ruled by the Spirit of God through your spirit and thus bring the entire body into subjection to God's will. Mind exercises are intended to settle and focus the mind and to fortify the mind against carnal suggestion. A believer who can filter out the carnal noise and intently focus on his spirit's pleading will have a significant advantage in bringing the whole body into subjection to the will of God. A mind that cannot focus on the spirit's voice will be prone to anxiety, depression, and sinful behavior.

Once a secure and settled mind has been obtained, the believer can effectively impose *mind frames* for the appropriate situations. The child of God learns to think and respond as Christ would if encountering the same circumstance. This is God-honoring, for the Father's ultimate goal for all believers is to be thoroughly conformed to the image of His Son (Rom. 8:29). When we obtain and submit to Christ-mindedness, we are Christlike. Thinking as Christ would think ensures the Holy Spirit will not be hindered from operation, thus allowing the free working of God through the believer. A surgeon inserts his hand into a latex glove before performing surgery to remove a cancerous tumor from his patient. The glove does not possess the power, wisdom, or the ability in and of itself to do anything, yet the glove is what grips the surgical instruments to accomplish the blessing. The glove and not the surgeon's hand is seen. In this way, an invisible God reaches His hand from heaven's glories through the believer's body to demonstrate His power and presence on earth. May our spirit, soul, and body be sanctified wholly for His good pleasure. May our minds not hinder what could be!

Appendix

The Mind and Heart

The Mind

W. E. Vine defines the various nouns and verbs rendered "mind" in the New Testament.

Mind – Nouns

1. *nous*, denotes, speaking generally, the seat of reflective consciousness, comprising the faculties of perception and understanding, and those of feeling, judging and determining.
2. *dianoia*, lit. "a thinking through, or over, a meditation, reflecting."
3. *ennoia*, "an idea, notion, intent."
4. *noema*, "thought, design."
5. *gnome*, "a purpose, judgment, opinion."
6. *phronema*, "what one has in the mind, the thought."

Mind - Verbs

1. *phroneo*, signifies (a) "to think, to be minded in a certain way"; (b) "to think of, be mindful of." It implies moral interest or reflection, not mere unreasoning opinion.
2. *anamimnesko*, "to remind, call to remembrance."

3. *hupomimnesko*, "to cause one to remember, put one in mind."

4. *hupotithemi*, lit., "to place under" (hupo, "under," tithemi, "to place"), ... also denotes "to suggest, put into one's mind."

5. *sophroneo*, signifies "to be of sound mind," or "in one's right mind, sober-minded."[1]

Although all of the above convey some facet of thinking, pondering, reflecting or contemplating, the most common Greek words translated "mind" in the New Testament are *nous* (occurring 24 times) and *dianoia* (occurring 12 times). These best express the meaning of the mind – "the seat of reflective consciousness, comprising the faculties of perception and understanding, and the ability to reason with rational thought."

Gerald Cowen comments regarding the Greek and Hebrew language limitations of the word "mind":

> ... the mind is considered to be the center of the person. However, in Scripture the heart is more often considered to be the center of the human personality. In the Old Testament, especially, this is true because of the lack of an exact equivalent for *mind*. The word *heart* fills this void, and the New Testament follows the practice of the Old Testament very closely. Why then can the mind as well as the heart be spoken of as the center of a person? Because in Hebrew thought a person is looked at as a single entity with no attempt to compartmentalize the person into separate parts which act more or less independently of one another. Therefore, the heart, mind, and soul, while in some ways different, are seen as one. The mind is portrayed oftentimes, especially in the New Testament, as the center of a person's ethical nature. The mind can be evil. It is described as "reprobate" (Rom. 1:28),

"fleshly" (Col. 2:18), vain (Eph. 4:17), corrupt (1 Tim. 6:5; 2 Tim. 3:8), and defiled (Titus 1:15). On the other hand, three Gospels command us to love God with "all" our mind (Matt. 22:37; Mk. 12:30; Lk. 10:27). This is possible because the mind can be revived and empowered by the Holy Spirit (Rom. 12:2) and because God's laws under the new covenant are put into our minds (Heb. 8:10; 10:16).[2]

The Heart

Beside being a critical organ for physical life, the "heart" (*kardia*) is employed in the New Testament to identify the inner man's mental and moral activity; both the rational and the emotional aspects are included. *Kardia* is translated "heart" 160 out of 161 occurrences in the New Testament. *Psushe*, the normal word for "soul," is rendered once as "heart" (Eph. 6:6), but normally these terms are not interchangeable in the New Testament. When moral character and issues of personal life are the specific context of the passage, it is best to refer to the "heart" rather than to speak more generally of the "soul." 1 Corinthians 7:37 confirms that the "heart" has influence over "the will" (the desires of self-consciousness within the soul): *"Nevertheless he that standeth steadfast in his heart, having no necessity, but hath power over his own will, and hath so decreed in his heart that he will keep his virgin, doeth well."*

What does the "heart" of man refer to? Certainly the heart organ may be referred to, but more generally the "heart" refers to an invisible component of the human soul relating to emotions, desires, moral inclinations and cognitive abilities. Figuratively, the heart is the hidden spring of the personal and inward life. According to Scripture, the heart contains the following inward life components:

Emotions

Grief (Jn. 14:1; Rom. 9:2; 2 Cor. 2:4)
Joy (Jn. 16:22; Eph. 5:19)
Affections (Lk. 24:32; Acts 21:13)
Faith (Mk. 11:23; Rom. 10:10; Heb. 3:12)

The Will

The source of desires (Matt. 5:28; 2 Pet. 2:14)
The will (Rom. 6:17; Col. 3:15)
Intentions (Heb. 4:12)
Purpose (Acts 11:23; 2 Cor. 9:7)

Moral Inclinations

Naturally Depraved (Matt. 15:19; Jer. 17:9)

Affected by the Conscience (Acts 2:37; 1 Jn. 3:20)

Cognitive Abilities

Perception (Jn. 12:40; Eph. 4:18)
Understanding (Matt. 13:15; Rom. 1:21)
Thinking (Matt. 9:4; Heb. 4:12)
Reasoning powers (Mk. 2:6; Lk. 24:38)
Imagination (Lk. 1:51)

Endnotes

Introduction to Mind Frames
1. Watchman Nee, *Vol. 1 – The Spiritual Man* (Christian Fellowship Publishers, New York: 1969) p. 27

God's Icon
1. Trent C. Butler, *Holman Bible Dictionary* – Image of God: Persons as Body-Soul (Holman Bible Publishers – electronic copy)
2. Watchman Nee, op. cit., Vol. 1, p. 24

Dividing Asunder Soul and Spirit
1. *Holman's Bible Dictionary*, op. cit., Anthropology
2. Edythe Draper, *Draper's Quotations from the Christian World* – Soul (Tyndale House Publishers Inc., Wheaton, Il. – electronic copy)
3. David Bercot, *A Dictionary of Early Christian Beliefs* (Hendrickson Publishers, Peabody, MA 1998) p. 624
4. C.I. Scofield, *The New Scofield Study Bible* (Oxford University Press, New York: 1967), p. 1293
5. David Bercot, op. cit., pp. 624-626
6. Ibid., p. 625

Man "with Christ"
1. Ibid., p. 627

A Perfect Heart and a Willing Mind

1. Ibid., p. 624
2. William MacDonald, *Believer's Bible Commentary* (Thomas Nelson Publishers, Nashville, TN: 1989), p.1288
3. John Grassmick, *The Bible Knowledge Commentary – New Testament,* ed. John Walvoord and Roy Zuck (Victor Books, Wheaton IL: 1983), p. 124
4. Figure adapted from Microsoft clipart (Microsoft Pub 97, Microsoft Corp.:1991-1996).

Mental Fitness

1. Texe Marrs, *New Age Cults and Religions* (Living Truth Publishers, Austin TX: 1990), p. 69
2. Ibid. p. 67
3. Warren Wiersbe, *The Bible Exposition Commentary, Vol. 2* (Victor Books, Wheaton, IL: 1989), pp. 327-328
4. Dr. Howard Taylor, *Spiritual Secret of Hudson Taylor* (Whitaker House, New Kensington, PA: 1996), p. 351
5. Lyle Dorsett, *The Life of D.L. Moody A Passion For Souls* (Moody Press, Chicago: 1997) pp. 151-152
6. Warren Wiersbe, op. cit., p. 622
7. William MacDonald, op. cit., p. 2254

The Mental Battlefield

1. *Demon Experiences A Compilation* (Tyndale House Publishers, Wheaton, IL: 1972) pp. 11, 45, 87, 106, 114
2. Watchman Nee, op. cit., Vol. 1, p. 177
3. Matthew Henry, *Matthew Henry's Commentary on the Whole Bible* (Electronic Edition STEP Files Copyright © 1998, Parsons Technology, Inc), Jas. 4:7
4. Ibid., Acts 5:3

The Mental Battlefield (cont.)

5. Stanley D. Toussaint, *The Bible Knowledge Commentary – New Testament* (Victor Books, Wheaton, IL), p. 365
6. Warren Wiersbe, op. cit., p. 421
7. Watchman Nee, op. cit., Vol. 3, p. 15

Spiritual Mind Frames

1. *Streams in the Desert*, March 13, pp.112-113
2. David Bercot, op. cit., p. 427
3. Dr. Howard Taylor, op. cit., p. 262
4. Bob Laurent, Watchman Nee (Barbour Publishing, Inc. Uhrichsville, OH), p. 79
5. W. Grinton Berry, *Foxe's Book of Martyrs* (Power Books, Old Tappen, New Jersey), p. 9
6. Warren Wiersbe, op. cit., Vol. 1, p. 108
7. Bob Laurent, op. cit., p. 134
8. Dr. Howard Taylor, op. cit., p. 368
9. Warren Wiersbe, op. cit., Vol. 1, p. 416
10. Miriam Taylor Wert, *The Spirit of the Shepherd* (Evangel USA: 1999) p. 42
11. Dr. Howard Taylor, op. cit., p. 273
12. Ibid., p. 275
13. Ibid., p. 282
14. *Draper's Quotations from the Christian World, op. cit,.* – Memory (Isaac Asimov)
15. Bob Laurent, op. cit., p.36
16. Warren Wiersbe, op. cit., Vol. 1, p. 238

A Mind Set upon Christ

1. Warren Wiersbe, op. cit., Vol. 1, p. 117
2. Ibid., p. 296
3. Dr. Howard Taylor, op. cit., pp. 262-263

The Blessed Mind of Christ

1. G. H. Lang, *Anthony Norris Groves* (The Paternoster Press, London: 1949), p. 197
2. Warren Wiersbe, op. cit., Vol. 2, p. 69

Appendix

1. *Vine's Expository Dictionary of Biblical Words* (Thomas Nelson Publishers – electronic copy: 1985)
2. *Holman's Bible Dictionary*, op. cit., Mind